Light Forensics

Copyright ©: Steven Magee 2014

Edition 1.1

Cover Picture: The Sun appears to have magnification, filtering, and interference effects when viewed through tri-focal glasses. Sunglasses, glasses and contact lenses modify the light that the eyes receive.

Light Forensics © Steven Magee

Contents

1. Introduction — Page 5
2. Toxic Light — Page 7
3. Sun — Page 9
4. Sunlight — Page 12
5. Modified Solar Radiation Spectrum — Page 17
6. Atmospheric Filtering — Page 18
7. Altitude — Page 22
8. Speed of Light — Page 29
9. Sunspots — Page 30
10. Blue Sky — Page 34
11. Nighttime — Page 47
12. Aurora — Page 49
13. Moonlight — Page 52
14. Starlight — Page 53
15. Comets — Page 54
16. Solar Radiation & Weather — Page 56
17. High Cirrus — Page 64
18. Chemtrail Light — Page 68
19. Earthquake Light — Page 70
20. Volcanic Light — Page 75
21. Water Light — Page 80
22. Turbulent Light — Page 83
23. Reflected Light — Page 86
24. High Solar Radiation — Page 89
25. Tree Light — Page 91

26. Plant Light	Page 95
27. Fertility Light	Page 100
28. Farm Light	Page 102
29. Fossil Fuel Light	Page 104
30. Polluted Light	Page 107
31. Satellite Light	Page 115
32. Man-Made Reflections	Page 120
33. Structure Radiation	Page 121
34. Alternate Energy	Page 137
35. Glass	Page 145
36. Privacy Glass	Page 152
37. Window Coatings	Page 157
38. Roofs	Page 160
39. Air Conditioning	Page 162
40. Paints	Page 163
41. Ground Materials	Page 164
42. Architecture	Page 165
43. Homes	Page 168
44. Home Selection	Page 170
45. Cars	Page 175
46. Artificial Light	Page 178
47. Tanning Lamps and Beds	Page 188
48. Televisions, Computers & Phones	Page 190
49. Cinema Light	Page 194
50. VR Displays & Microscopes	Page 196
51. Strobe Light	Page 197
52. Flicker Light	Page 199
53. New Lighting	Page 201

54. Streetlights	Page 202
55. Gaslights & Flares	Page 207
56. Arc Welding	Page 209
57. Bedroom Light	Page 210
58. Food Spoilage by Light	Page 211
59. Colors & Moods	Page 213
60. Aggression	Page 216
61. Light Modulation	Page 221
62. Natural Light	Page 223
63. Lighting Levels	Page 227
64. Summary	Page 229
65. Definitions	Page 233
66. References	Page 236
67. Internet	Page 241
68. Acknowledgments	Page 242
69. About the Author	Page 243
70. Author Contact	Page 245
71. Book Reviews	Page 252

Light Forensics © Steven Magee

Introduction

Light Forensics is developed out of the book "Toxic Light". Light Forensics presents the various forms of light that were discussed in Toxic Light for those who want to diagnose problematic lighting environments. The field of light forensics is relatively new and is currently rapidly developing. Toxic Light is an expanded version of this book and has additional information in it regarding the human health aspects of light.

Toxic light is a new field of research into human health. Can light really be toxic? Yes, and it may be the driving force behind much of the illness and disease in modern society. This book could potentially save your life and drastically improve your health and mind.

We will take a look into the various forms of light and assess them for their ability to impact health. Something as simple as your household lighting may be able to affect you. Random aches and pains, skin problems, tiredness or insomnia? It may be the light in your environment.

Light is one of the least understood aspects of nature and arguably the most important. We will start out by examining sunlight and then move onto the many sources of artificial light that are present today. Light is almost everywhere and we will see that it has many different forms, even though they look the same to the human eye. We will look into the health aspects of light and how it may be affecting you.

We will investigate the amount of daily natural light that your body needs to be healthy and you may be surprised by the type of light that you need and also the number of hours of exposure that we come up with. By the end of the book you will have a good understanding of the different types of lighting and most importantly, the types of lighting to avoid.

Diagrams and photographs are used to illustrate many of the concepts of the book. If you are reading this in black and white, then descriptions of the pictures accompany them to explain the concepts. The contents of the book should be accessible to most people through the visual explanations of subjects discussed in the book.

This book is aimed at the general public, the medical profession, and the engineering profession. Mathematics is avoided and the book presents the health concepts of the various forms of light in a readable format to the general public. Important points are in bold font.

This book contains the very latest research on light and the human environment. It should be viewed as the current ideas on a new branch of scientific study and the contents are subject to review by the scientific community. The author and publisher accept no liability whatsoever for any of the contents and the book is published in the spirit of unrestricted access to the latest ideas and scientific theories in a changing world. You should always consult with a licensed and certified medical professional on any aspects of health, sickness or disease.

"Sunlight is more powerful than any drug; it is safe, effective, and available free of charge. If it could be patented, it would be hyped as the greatest medical breakthrough in history. It's that good."

Mike Adams

Light Forensics © Steven Magee

Toxic Light

Potentially toxic light is almost everywhere in modern society:

- Artificial street lighting.
- Artificial home lighting.
- Artificial office lighting.
- Anywhere where there is glass.
- In your car.
- In your home.
- In your office.
- Televisions of every type.
- Computer monitors of every type.
- At sunrise.
- At sunset.
- Near the north and south poles.
- In any large city.
- In chemical trails from aircraft.
- In polluted atmosphere.
- Anywhere where the tree canopy is not present.

So what may toxic light be shown to do in the future? In the future the following conditions may be proven to be related to toxic light:

- Cancer.

- Depression.
- Heart attacks.
- Circulation issues.
- Diabetes.
- Brain and nerve issues.
- Disruption of circadian rhythm.
- General aches and pains.
- Bone issues.
- Aggression.
- Psychiatric problems.
- Almost any of the current medical problems in society may be related to toxic light.

"We estimate that vitamin D deficiency is the most common medical condition in the world."
Dr. Michael F. Holick

Light Forensics © Steven Magee

Sun

Our closest star at just 93 million miles from Earth. A giant nuclear reactor that appears at sunrise every day, warms us and gives light to our lives until sunset. It does this every day without fail.

The Sun is so close to us that we can tap into its nuclear energy through the light and warmth that it radiates. Solar power technology has matured and we are now starting to widely use this resource for our energy needs.

The Sun sends us approximately 1,366 watts per square meter (W/m^2) of energy to the Earth and we call this "irradiance", the measure of solar radiation power. We lose some of this energy through atmospheric effects, such as scattering and absorption. By the time it gets to sea level in the tropics, about 17% of the energy has disappeared if the Sun was directly overhead, also called "Zenith". We now have about 1,130 watts per square meter left of the energy and this is a high amount of power.

The Sun is only directly overhead at the tropics in summertime. Any places outside of the tropics will never see the Sun at zenith. Instead it will be at a lower angle and we need to know how this affects the energy it creates at ground level. We need to introduce a concept called "Air Mass".

Air mass is a measurement of how thick the atmosphere is when looking at an astronomical object. In our case we are interested in the Sun.

If you increase air mass then you will reduce the power level due to the solar radiation passing through more of the atmosphere. Air mass increases as you head towards the poles and this will cause a reduction in power received from the Sun at sea level. Air mass will change with the seasons and the two extremes for air mass will be winter solstice and summer solstice when outside of the tropics.

Light Forensics © Steven Magee

So our average irradiance at sea level is 1,130 W/m^2 in the tropics, or is it? Actually, no. There is another factor to consider: Reflections. Reflections can cause irradiance to increase significantly. There are many types of reflections that can increase irradiance and we will look into these in later chapters. "Albedo" is the correct name for this effect.

So is this the only power increase? No, we have another: Altitude. The higher up we get into the sky from sea level, the less atmosphere that the Sun's rays have to pass through to reach the ground. So we will be able to receive more than 1,130 W/m^2 on average at higher elevations when the Sun is at zenith.

So is this it? No, there is another: Atmospherics. The atmosphere can vary in its transparency. Sometimes more energy will arrive at the ground from Space and at other times it will be less. It all depends on the atmosphere and its content, such as dust and pollution.

So as you can see, solar radiation power is a complex equation of items that can affect irradiance values and these values are always changing based on the environment and weather.

When we measure irradiance over a time period, such as a day, we call this "Insolation". Insolation is usually quoted in watts per square meter per day. The National Renewable Energy Laboratory (NREL) has produced many graphs that show insolation values around the world. Knowing insolation values is very useful in calculating the solar radiation power levels over the year in locations around the Earth.

This book is aimed at increasing awareness of these factors so that you can make informed decisions about solar radiation power and how it interacts with human health. We will now look into the various factors that you should know about.

"The Sun is the cosmological phenomenon which is mainly responsible for what the world has become and it would be impossible to remove from the skies without ending the existences of most of all living beings in the same process."

Unknown

Light Forensics © Steven Magee

Sunlight

Sunlight is made up of lots of photons that were generated at the Sun in nuclear reactions. A photon has some of the properties of a wave and some of the properties of a particle. Photons are energy and humans know this energy as sunburn (ultraviolet), light (visible) and heat (infrared).

Sunlight can have polarity. This can occur when it passes through a filter or is reflected from a surface. Most humans will know light polarization as a type of sunglasses that can be purchased. These cut down on reflections (glare) from surfaces and bodies of water by using a polarized filter coating.

Light comes in many forms. Some of these are parallel light, semi-parallel light, non-parallel light, diffracted light and interference light. Basically sunlight travels in parallel, semi-parallel light is directional light that has started to scatter and non-parallel light is scattered light that travels in all directions. Diffracted light occurs when the light passes over an object which causes spreading light waves to occur and interference light is made up of spreading light waves that have started to cross into each other and interact.

Parallel light is produced by the Sun and is generally referred to by optical engineers as collimated light. A direct view of the Sun's disk in the sky is parallel light. Sunlight is regarded as powerful and in the wrong situation it can be harmful to human health. Most people will be familiar with the medical advice to not look directly at the Sun. The Sun is very powerful when viewed directly with the human eye. If the Sun is reflected from a flat mirror or precision engineered flat surface, this reflection is still parallel due to the Sun's shape still being visible.

Semi-parallel light is a directional form of light that has some scattering in it. An image cannot be seen but it has maintained its ability to be directed. It is a powerful reflection.

Light Forensics © Steven Magee

The Sun reflecting off water would be a good description of this type of light.

Non-parallel light is scattered light that travels in random directions. This is the desirable configuration of light sources for humans. No image of the original source of light can be seen nor are there any bright patches of reflected sunlight.

If the Sun is reflected from a surface that scatters light and the Sun cannot be seen, then this is semi-parallel or non-parallel light.

Diffraction is caused by obstacles in the path of the parallel light. The Sun can be seen to bleed into the object when it is photographed. It shows up in photographs as a light source at the center with lines coming out of it. The amount of lines coming out depends on the amount of diffraction taking place.

The best way to describe interference light is to direct you to images of light. Interference light shows up as rings around light sources and interference patterns of bright patches of light when light sources are photographed. This can commonly be seen when watching movies of pop concerts.

Diffraction and interference effects are what the forest canopy produces.

A diagram of how the interference effect is formed from light waves intersecting can be found in the next diagram. The light waves encounter an obstacle or object and this causes diffraction. Diffraction just means that the light waves have started to spread outwards from the obstacle. Interference occurs when the spreading waves start interacting with each other.

Light Forensics © Steven Magee

Interference Diagram

The light waves arrive in parallel and expand outwards when they pass through the two apertures. Interference is produced where the waves intersect. This is seen as the bright and dark bands on the right. The dark is destructive and the bright is constructive interference.

For more information on interference:
http://electron9.phys.utk.edu/optics421/modules/m5/Interference.htm

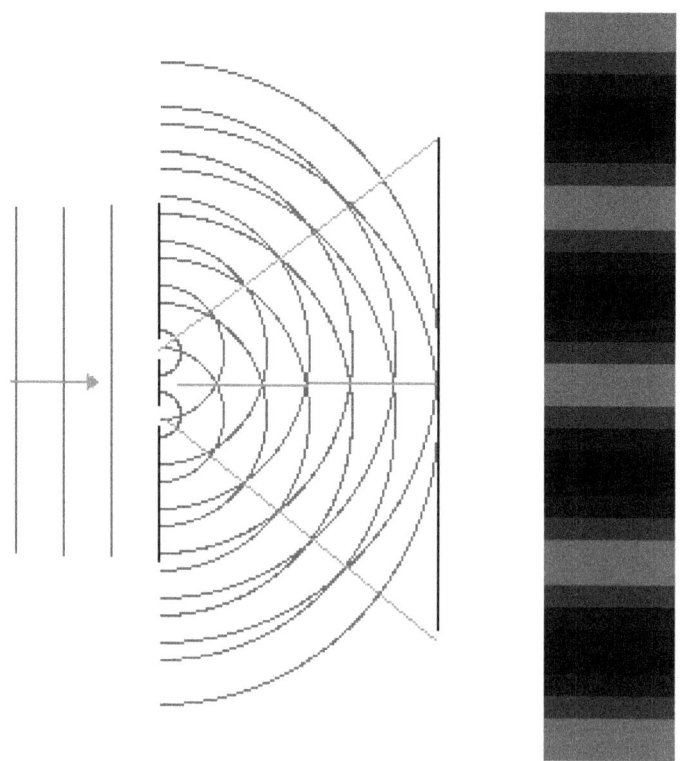

Light Forensics © Steven Magee

Solar radiation is broad spectrum radiation. This means that it contains many different types of frequencies of energy. The largest sources of energy are:

- Ultraviolet (UV).
- Optical (Visible).
- Infrared (IR).

In addition to these it contains other frequencies of energy, many of which are not effectively documented by the medical profession. The effects of the content of broad spectrum solar radiation on the human mind and body are not fully understood. Until broad spectrum solar radiation is understood, it pays to exercise caution around it.

The power levels of ground based solar radiation are not too different from that of Space. The atmosphere only absorbs about seventeen percent of the Space solar radiation energy at zenith. The frequency spectrum of the ground based solar radiation is very similar to that of Space with a just a few of the frequencies that are contained in the solar radiation spectrum being largely absorbed by the atmosphere.

The next diagram shows the solar radiation spectrum power levels.

"No life at all would be possible on this planet without the Sun...To teach people to be afraid of the Sun is harmful health advice that will ultimately kill more people than it saves. Most people have too little sunlight, not too much."

Mike Adams

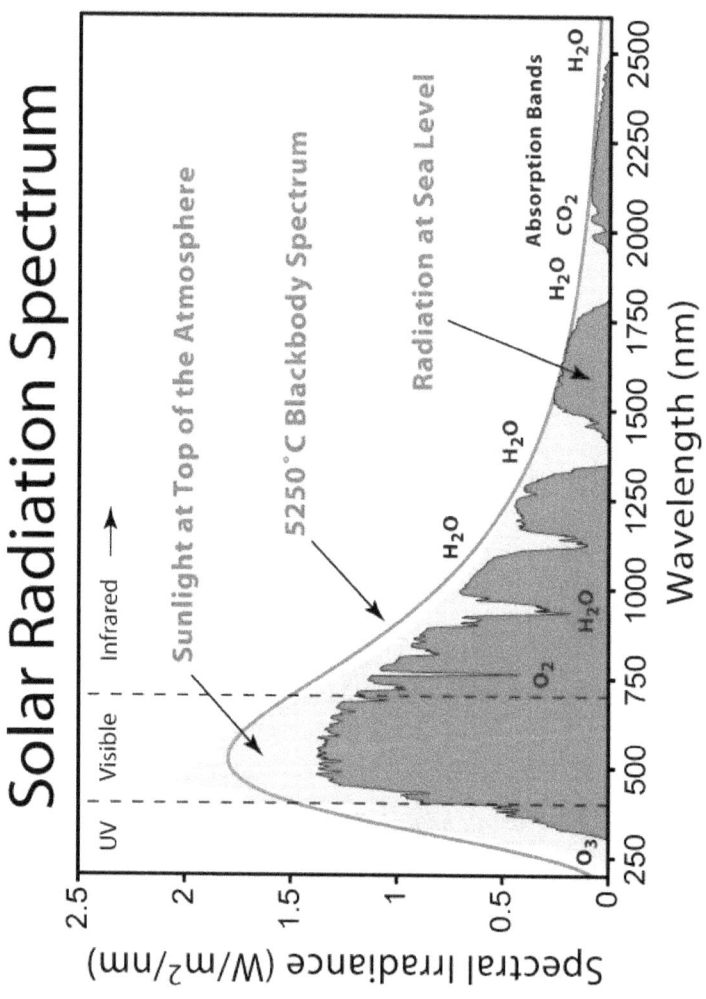

Modified Solar Radiation Spectrum

As we saw from the solar radiation spectrum graph, solar radiation is made up of many different forms of energy that make up the spectrum of solar radiation. This spectrum can be modified in a number of ways:

- Filtering.
- Diffraction and interference effects.
- Reflections.

Filtering is what happens when solar radiation passes through something like the atmosphere, clouds, water or glass. Filtering will remove certain elements of the solar radiation spectrum and may reduce the power levels of those that pass through the filter. The result is a different spectrum of solar radiation of a lower overall power level.

Diffraction and interference effects may remove some parts of the spectrum and replace them with newly created spectrum elements from the interference effects. Interference may also increase energy levels in certain parts of the spectrum while reducing it in others.

Reflected solar radiation will take on the properties of the material that reflected it. It will be a highly modified solar radiation spectrum in general. The most harmful form of light to the human appears to be spectrum modified light.

"Freedom is the open window through which pours the sunlight of the human spirit and human dignity."
Herbert Hoover

Light Forensics © Steven Magee

Atmospheric Filtering

A significant trend seems to be forming from global warming and this appears to be extreme seasons. Many places are now breaking their summer weather peak records and the same places are breaking their winter minimum records. Why would this be?

It seems that the large amount of gasses in the atmosphere get heated in summertime by solar radiation absorption due to the increased level of molecules that are present when compared to the past. This increases the ability for the atmosphere to absorb more water vapor and it does so. The extra molecules added to the atmosphere by the water vapor further reinforces the heating effects taking place by the solar radiation absorption.

We need to be very careful about letting the atmosphere heat up, as this gives the molecules more energy. They will move faster and some of them may eventually start escaping into Space. We do not want the atmosphere to heat up to a level where this may start happening. The other problem is that energetic molecule movement in the atmosphere will generate turbulence which will affect the solar radiation transmission through it.

In wintertime, everything cools down and condenses into clouds. The clouds reflect the solar radiation back into Space and prevent heating of the atmosphere and the ground. A net energy loss is the result as well as colder ground temperatures. Increasing snow, hail, and rain levels should be expected in wintertime.

Widening of the annual minimum and maximum temperatures is extremely undesirable and who knows where this will lead to if effective efforts are not taken to fix climate change soon.

The closer to the poles you live, the more atmospheric filtering of solar radiation that takes place. This is due to the air mass being higher nearer to the poles. Air mass is a measurement of the thickness of air that the solar radiation has to pass through. The larger the number, the thicker the air is. Let us see what 42 degrees latitude gives for air mass:

At summertime we have to subtract 23.5 degrees from the latitude for summer solstice:

Air mass =1/cos (42-23.5 degrees) = 1.05 air mass at summer.

In spring and autumn we use the latitude of 42 degrees:

Air mass =1/cos (42 degrees) = 1.35 air mass at spring/autumn.

Now let us add in 23.5 degrees to the equation for winter solstice:

Air mass = 1/cos (42+23.5 degrees) = 2.41 air mass in winter.

As we can see, air mass increases significantly in winter time. Winter has a 2.29 increase in air mass when compared to the summer, it more than doubles. Seasonal Affect Disorder Syndrome (SADS) appears to be global position dependent with almost none at the equator and increases to a high prevalence near to the poles. It appears to be the atmospheric filtering of the solar radiation that causes Seasonal Affect Disorder syndrome (SADS) and wintertime vitamin D deficiency.

Given the large number of people who appear to be affected during wintertime in these locations nearer to the poles, we can assume that there is something going on regarding human health in these locations. It is possible that the atmospheric pollution has made some of these locations optically toxic to humans during wintertime.

Light Forensics © Steven Magee

The effect is much worse the closer you get to the poles, as the air mass increases. At the poles it can be at the maximum value of approximately 38 all day long. If the solar radiation is biologically toxic at this air mass, you would not want to be in this location.

It has been known for a long time that colors can affect your mood. Now that the sunsets have turned orange and red, let us see what these colors produce in the human:

- Orange: Daring, stimulating.
- Red: Stimulating, excitement, anger.

It is recommended that you stay indoors during the time of the sunrise and sunsets. Watching the sky at this time may have long term health implications from toxic light exposure.

In places that are nearer to the polar regions the Sun does not rise above the horizon very far. At these locations, there is a high level of atmospheric filtration taking place on the solar radiation during the daytime. Given the levels of pollution in the atmosphere, winter sunlight may be bad for human health due to this level of filtration. Indeed, the increased filtering of winter sunlight may be driving the extreme winter conditions that we now see developing around the world.

Air mass varies with the seasons and also the location on the Earth. Within the tropics, air mass will reach its maximum power value of 1 during summertime. Air mass 1 corresponds to the Sun being directly overhead, air mass increases as the Sun moves from directly overhead down to the horizon. The Sun at the horizon gives an air mass of approximately 38.

Locations that are at or near air mass 1 in summertime in the USA are all Hawaiian islands, Florida and Texas. In summertime the air mass will move closer to 1 in the continental USA.

Air mass varies with solar elevation and atmospheric pollution levels. This is what Wikipedia lists the air mass (AM) and solar radiation energy content as with varying solar elevations, as referenced to zenith.

Space = AM0, $1367 W/m^2$

0° = AM1, $840 W/m^2$ to $1130 W/m^2$ (Solar noon at the equator during the equinox)

23° = AM1.09, $800 W/m^2$ to $1110 W/m^2$

30° = AM1.15, $780 W/m^2$ to $1100 W/m^2$

45° = AM1.41, $710 W/m^2$ to $1060 W/m^2$

48.2° = AM1.5, $680 W/m^2$ to $1050 W/m^2$

60° = AM2, $560 W/m^2$ to $970 W/m^2$

70° = AM2.9, $430 W/m^2$ to $880 W/m^2$

75° = AM3.8, $330 W/m^2$ to $800 W/m^2$

80° = AM5.6, $200 W/m^2$ to $660 W/m^2$

85° = AM10, $85 W/m^2$ to $480 W/m^2$

90° = AM38, $20 W/m^2$ (Sunrise & sunset)

You will note that there is low energy near sunrise and sunset and you will find very little ultraviolet (UV) content at that time. UV levels are considered to be extremely low within 45 minutes of these times. This fact is well known by sun-gazers who stare at the Sun during these times for health purposes. I do not recommend sungazing at orange or red sunsets, as there may be long term toxic light issues.

"Excess generally causes reaction, and produces a change in the opposite direction, whether it be in the seasons, or in individuals, or in governments."

Plato

Light Forensics © Steven Magee

Altitude

I have a lot of experience with altitude. I spent three years working at approximately 7,775 feet followed by five years at 13,796 feet and three more years at 6,875 feet. Altitude sickness is very real and the effects that it can have on people are diverse. Feeling faint is a common symptom and I have seen people actually faint at altitude.

When I worked in La Palma in the Canary Islands at 7,775 feet, the observatory was significantly above the tree line. The tree line is located at a very definite altitude. Above it, the vegetation significantly changes to low bushy growth of only a couple of feet tall. The trees at the tree line tend to be disfigured and showing stress. This indicates that the biological environment has changed and is biologically harmful to trees. It is likely a solar radiation effect.

The Hawaii observatory was significantly higher at 13,796 feet. It was a barren place with almost no visible life where the observatory was located. Just lots of rocks and cinder! It was far above the tree line. Our blood oxygen levels would be running at 80% of normal up there.

The Arizona observatory at 6,875 feet was below the tree line. However, it appeared to be high enough to cause growth defects in the trees. I remember the trees up there being twisted and disfigured. You could definitely feel the altitude sickness even at this lower elevation.

Altitude sickness is known to occur in most people above 4,900 feet. Aircraft commonly pressurize their cabins to the air pressure found at 6,900 feet to try and prevent these symptoms from occurring. However, some people still report altitude sickness symptoms at this pressure. They are probably the ones that you see holding the sick bags! Nausea is a feature of altitude sickness.

There are very definite symptoms that are associated with the different levels of altitude and Wikipedia states:

- *High altitude 1,500 to 3,500 metres (4,900 to 11,500 ft) - The onset of physiological effects of diminished inspiratory oxygen pressure (PiO2) includes decreased exercise performance and increased ventilation (lower arterial PCO2). Minor impairment exists in arterial oxygen transport (arterial oxygen saturation (SaO2) at least 90%), but arterial PO2 is significantly diminished. Because of the large number of people who ascend rapidly to altitudes between 2,400 and 4,000 m, high-altitude illness is common in this range.*

- *Very high altitude 3,500 to 5,500 metres (11,500 to 18,000 ft) - Maximum SaO2 falls below 90% as the arterial PO2 falls below 60mmHg. Extreme hypoxemia may occur during exercise, during sleep, and in the presence of high altitude pulmonary edema or other acute lung conditions. Severe altitude illness occurs most commonly in this range.*

- *Extreme altitude above 5,500 metres (18,000 ft) - Marked hypoxemia, hypocapnia, and alkalosis are characteristic of extreme altitudes. Progressive deterioration of physiologic function eventually outstrips acclimatization. As a result, no permanent human habitation occurs above 6,000m. A period of acclimatization is necessary when ascending to extreme altitude; abrupt ascent without supplemental oxygen for other than brief exposures invites severe altitude sickness.*

The Hawaii observatory was so high that we used to stop and acclimatize at 9,200 feet, before heading to the peak.

I was lucky enough to have two positions in Hawaii. The first position had me commuting from sea level to 13,796 feet on a daily basis. I would feel lethargic, have a headache, and show stomach problems during the day. In the evening, I just wanted to lay down and recover. I changed my position to the night shift and found that it was much more agreeable to human health. Indeed, it was one of my motivations to move onto the night shift. On nights you would stay on the mountain at 9,200 feet for five nights and commute up to 13,796 feet to work.

One of the things that I do remember that was distinct about working nights at 13,796 feet were the hallucinations. I saw some strange things on top of that mountain! I knew I was hallucinating and it was manageable feature of my job. I found it absolutely fascinating to see the tricks that the human mind could play on me. It was not often that I would have hallucinations, but it generally would occur on my first night on the mountain where my environmental conditions had been greatly changed.

Common to all three sites where I worked was that the long term staff appeared to get leg problems. Some of them would have very strange walks. Indeed, it was like being in the Monty Python's sketch of "The Ministry of Silly Walks"! It was as if their joints had gone stiff. They also did not appear to be very healthy. I suspect that it was caused by daily high altitude commuting and the strange environmental conditions that they were working in. This appears to be called "Delayed Radiation Myelopathy" and is well documented in the medical field of nuclear medicine.

I did see two of the long-term full-time mountain employees die of disease. These disease conditions that they had were preceded by many years of poor health. I imagine that high altitude commuting increases the risks of disease and premature death.

This leads me into the purpose of this chapter and that is as you increase in altitude, your environmental conditions significantly change. The higher you go, the greater the change is. There are a wide variety of changes that occur and we will look into these.

Temperature is the most obvious change. The higher you go, the cooler it gets. In Hawaii, you could be sunbathing in shorts on the beach in the morning and by afternoon you can be in your winter clothes making snowmen on top of the mountain!

Light Forensics © Steven Magee

The temperature change between sea level and 13,796 feet can be extreme. Less noticeable is the change in solar radiation levels. The sunlight is stronger and has frequencies of radiation in it that you will never find at sea level. As such, the solar radiation conditions are unnatural to the human. We see the effects of this at the tree line in the stressed trees.

Nighttime radiation levels are different also. Less atmospheric filtering is taking place and the radiation levels from Space are higher. You actually see less stars up there, due to the eyes being starved of oxygen. They lose some of their nighttime sensitivity.

The electrical conductivity of the air is very different. The air at altitude is in a partial vacuum and the density is far less. Nikola Tesla had noted during his research into wireless energy transmission that it was preferable to transmit at altitude due to the better conductivity of air to high electrical frequencies. He states that the conductivity was "better than copper wire". This electrical conductivity of the air increases exponentially with altitude.

The air is also electrically charged, as Wikipedia states: *Atmospheric electricity abounds in the environment; some traces of it are found less than four feet from the surface of the earth, but on attaining greater height it becomes more apparent. The main concept is that the air above the surface of the earth is usually, during fine weather, positively electrified, or at least that it is positive with respect to the Earth's surface, the Earth's surface being relatively negative. The measurements of atmospheric electricity can be seen as measurements of difference of potential between a point of the Earth's surface, and a point somewhere in the air above it. The atmosphere in different regions is often found to be at different local potentials, which differ from that of the ground sometimes even by as much as 3000 Volts within 100 feet (30 m).*

Pressure is less and your body has to work harder to extract oxygen from the thinner air. The body will create extra blood cells and the blood will thicken. Everything in your body will start to expand as the pressure reduces. Your body is constantly working to address these expansion issues. You will need to be drinking plenty of water and electrolytes to enable the body to adapt. The opposite effects occur as you descend to lower elevations.

As you can see, the environment at altitude is very different to what it is at sea level. For the purpose of human health, it appears that it is wise to work and live below 4,900 feet. Living and working above this altitude is likely to lead to altitude related health problems occurring. If you do work at altitude then daily commuting to altitude is undesirable and it is far better to stay there until your work is completed. You should probably not stay in a high altitude job for a long period of time and be aware that you are increasing your risks of illness, disease, cancer, and mental health problems in such jobs. Living and working near or above the tree line is not advisable.

You should only be living and working at altitude if you can trace your genetics to it. People in high cities such as La Paz, Bolivia, at an elevation of 11,942 ft will be genetically adapted to that area. For them, they would be wise to stay at that elevation.

Living at sea level may also be an issue today, particularly in or near to large coastal cities. Much of the pollution that is created by these will stay at sea level. The majority of pollutants are heavier than air and may stay near to the ground as they cool. This can be seen in large cities like Los Angeles as a cloud of pollution hanging over the city. It can also be seen near to erupting volcanoes.

If you live in locations such as these, it is advisable to live at an altitude that puts you above the pollution cloud. The ideal location for human health is not to actually live in such a polluted area.

The cloud of pollution over Los Angeles is shown in the next picture.

Light Forensics © Steven Magee

"Because of the high altitude, you get drunk really fast. So everyone's drunk all the time."

Clea Duvall

Light Forensics © Steven Magee

City Pollution

The band of atmospheric pollution hanging over Los Angeles, California, as viewed from the Griffith Observatory. Pollution will unnaturally filter light.

Speed of Light

The speed of light is regarded as 186,282 miles per hour in a vacuum. The interesting thing about the speed of light is that it slows down when it passes through any type of gas, liquid or solid. Of particular note is the speed at which it passes through glass. 1,260 hundred miles per hour is the approximate speed of light through glass.

The refractive index is a measure of how the speed of light is affected as it passes through a material. Glass has a refractive index of about 1.5, depending on the glass.

The formula for the refractive index is:

Refractive index = speed of light / speed of light through material

"Each ray of light moves in the coordinate system 'at rest' with the definite, constant velocity V independent of whether this ray of light is emitted by a body at rest or a body in motion."

Albert Einstein

Sunspots

Interference of solar radiation may be caused by sunspots. Dr. Maki Takota showed that the presence of sunspots was related to the formation of certain chemicals in the blood. He also was able to relate blood chemistry to eclipses, solar flares, and sunrises.

A.L. Tchijevsky, a Russian professor, found a correlation between sunspot activity and human behavior. He linked major world events to the cycles of the sunspots! Generally, unrest was linked to sunspot maximum.

Sunspot minimum was linked to the occurrence of diseases in society by Professor d'Arsonval and others. It is not just human disease, crop production is affected too! Crops have a lower yield generally in sunspot minimum periods.

We really should not be surprised that sunspots can create changes in the human mind and body, as we have lived in the presence of the Sun for many thousands of years.

Sunspots do not cause much of a variance in solar irradiance levels from the Sun, typically oscillating up and down by just 1 watt per meter squared. It does not sound like much, but over the surface of the Earth, it is a huge amount of energy! The sunspot cycle is approximately eleven years and has been extensively studied by astronomers. The picture on the next page shows the sunspot cycle and how the power levels vary.

Light Forensics © Steven Magee

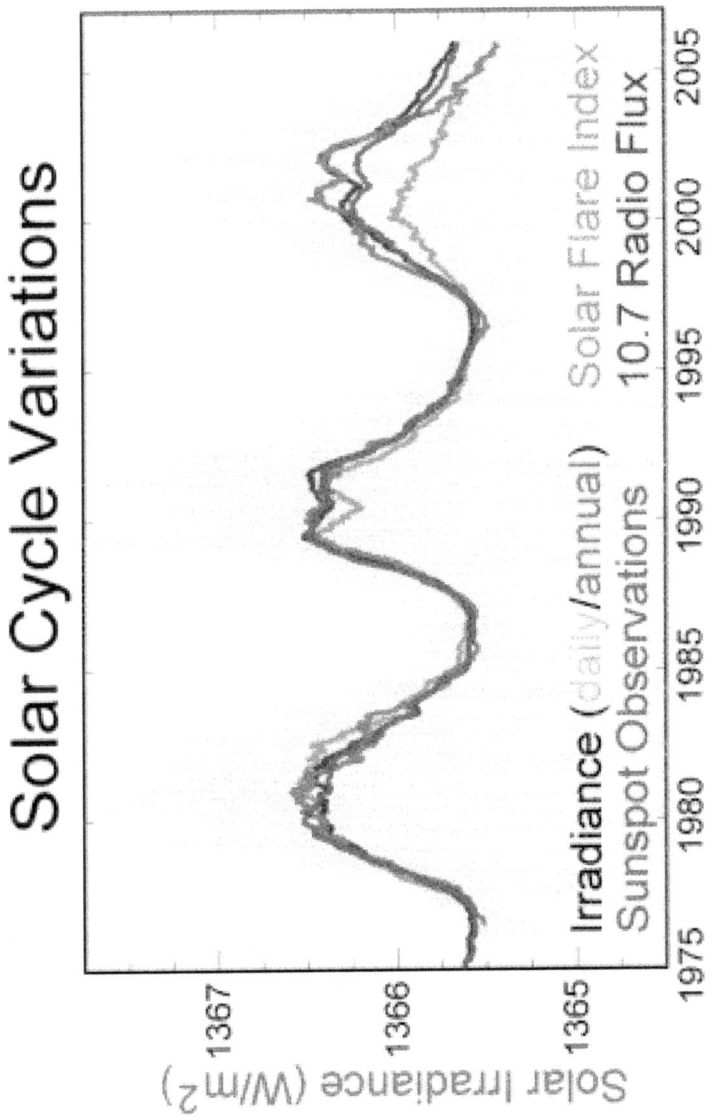

Unfortunately, it appears that little attention was paid to the sunspot effect during the development of the Space industry. We now have an Earth that has thousands of man-made satellites circling it. Every time one of these passes in front of the Sun, it creates a man-made Sun spot! The effects of this are currently unknown on the human mind and body, and the natural world. An asteroid going into orbit around the Earth would have comparable effects.

A concerning problem is the build up of Space debris that is now in orbit around the Earth. The Space industry has put massive amounts of debris in orbit around the Earth and it is the pinnacle of human pollution. This Space debris may be creating electromagnetic radiation interference and possibly induction effects into the Earth below. If it grows sufficiently in quantity, it may even start to electromagnetically shield the Earth!

Aircraft create an eclipse when they pass in front of the Sun. Unfortunately, they also leave a chemical trail behind them that may linger for hours. The chemical trail will act as a filter to the sunlight and may also create shadowing, polarization, diffraction and interference effects.

Dr. Abraham Hoffer was able to link the human mental state to sunlight and, in particular, the equinoxes and solstices. He found that mental functioning peaks in January and July, and normalizes after March and September.

The following diagram shows satellite or airplane solar interference effects.

"If I had to choose a religion, the Sun as the universal giver of life would be my God."
Napoleon Bonaparte

Light Forensics © Steven Magee

Satellite Interference

Sunspots, Mercury, Venus, the Moon, man-made satellites, Space debris, airplanes, chemical trails, and pollution all appear to have the ability to interfere with solar radiation transmission and create interference radiation waves.

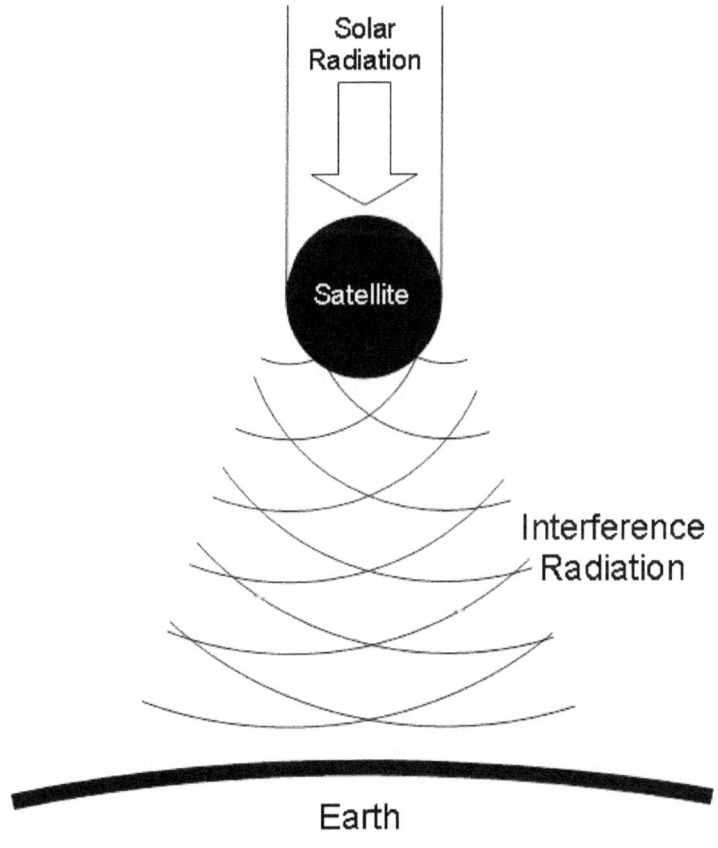

Light Forensics © Steven Magee

Blue Sky

Why is the sky blue? Astronomers say that it is because blue light scatters more than red. This theory was developed by Baron Raleigh. Wikipedia states the following: *John William Strutt, 3rd Baron Rayleigh, OM (12 November 1842 – 30 June 1919) was an English physicist who, with William Ramsay, discovered the element argon, an achievement for which he earned the Nobel Prize for Physics in 1904. He also discovered the phenomenon now called Rayleigh scattering, explaining why the sky is blue, and predicted the existence of the surface waves now known as Rayleigh waves.*

So, for over a hundred years, light scattering by air molecules is why we think the sky is blue!

The following pages show this effect.

This is how the spectrum scatters according to the wavelength of light.

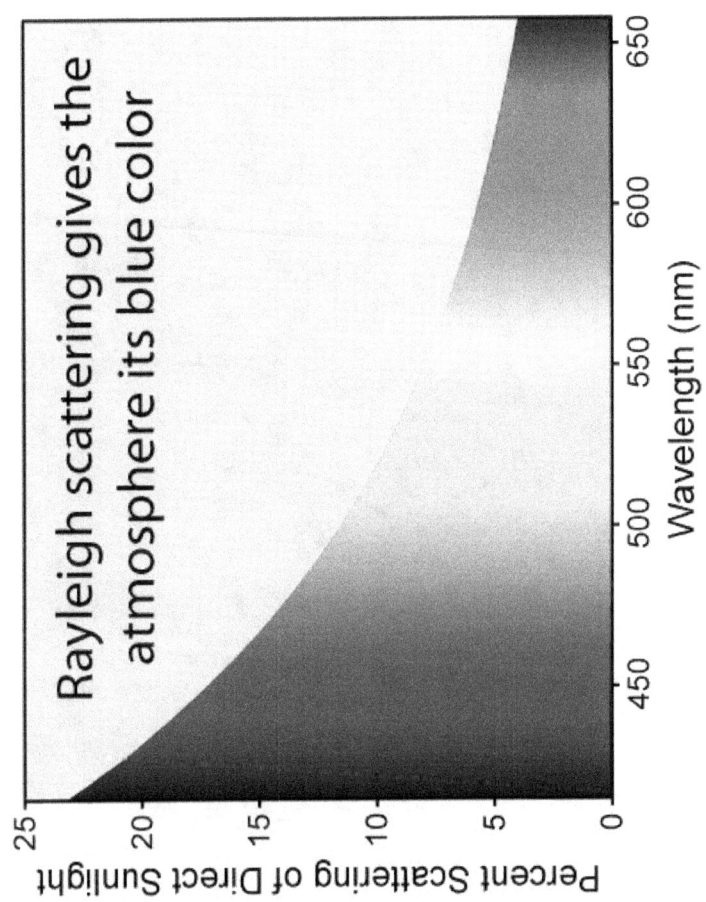

Light Forensics © Steven Magee

Here is the blue sky spectrum.

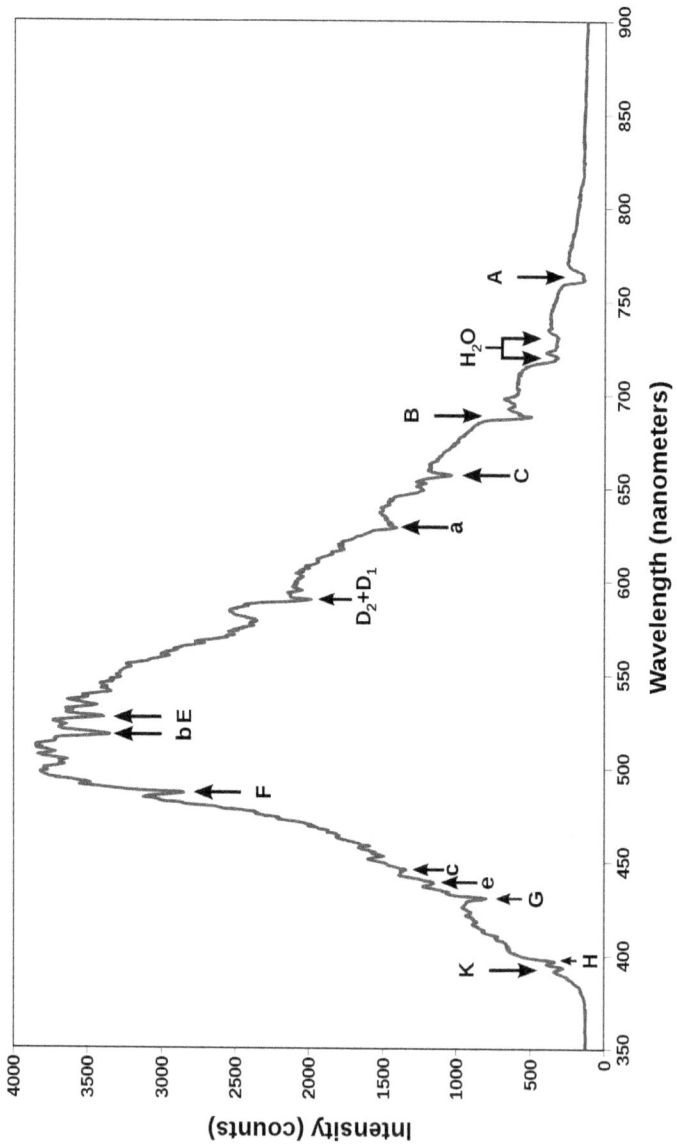

Light Forensics © Steven Magee

The sky is a much lighter blue at horizon than at higher elevations at noon.

Obscuring the direct view of the Sun with a cactus shows us that the white light of the Sun extends only for a short distance around the Sun. The rest of the sky is uniformly blue.

Light Forensics © Steven Magee

At sunset we can observe the blue sky turning off. The planets and stars are visible, even though it is still light out.

Light Forensics © Steven Magee

Are you convinced? The interesting thing is that I am not. The theory does not appear to hold up today for the following reasons:

- When looking down from Space we do not see blue against the white, green, and brown background of the surface of the Earth.
- When looking up at the Moon we see a white moon, not a blue moon during daytime. The moon is 1/500,000 as bright as the Sun.
- When looking down in a plane at 35,000 feet, we see the Earth's surface looking normal, not blue tinted.
- When looking up in a plane at 35,000 feet we see blue sky.
- Concord flew at 60,000 feet and the sky was still blue above it and the ground was still the same colors.
- Space appears black at 100,000 feet when looking up. The ground still appears to be its normal colors when looking down. Looking sideways reveals a blue colored atmospheric layer.
- The blue sky color is created near to the edge of Space and there are very few air molecules up there to scatter the light.
- Water molecules appear to absorb light, just leaving blue penetrating to the deeper levels. That is why the objects in the ocean appear blue when scuba diving in the deep.
- If scattering was the cause of blue sky, then it would be very prevalent at sea level and at the horizon where the scattering would be predominant due to the amount of air molecules present. It is not the case.
- Sunlight appears to scatter into white light. This can be seen to occur in the middle of the day when looking towards the horizon, where scattering would be predominant due to the amount of air molecules present.

It can be seen to occur when smoke particles are present from forest fires and clouds also exhibit the white scattered light effect.

- The blue sky would not be uniform in color, it would vary significantly.
- The Sun would appear to be yellow, orange, or red at solar noon.

If it is not scattering, then what is it? I believe it is a low level of glow caused by excitation of high altitude air molecules by solar radiation absorption. The reason for this is:

- During daytime the Earth faces the largest nuclear reactor in the solar system, called the Sun.
- During the daytime the Earth is facing the solar wind.
- The upper atmosphere absorbs microwaves, ultraviolet, X-rays, and gamma rays. This is energy.
- From the observations of St. Elmo's fire, we know that air molecules glow blue when excited by energy.
- From observations of nuclear energy, we know that water molecules glow blue due to Cherenkov radiation. Water molecules are present in the atmosphere in the form of vapor.
- We extensively use gas lighting products in industry. Gas lighting simply excites gas with energy to emit light.
- The electrical industry has extensively documented the blue glow of air at near vacuum inside electrical valves.
- We know that the radiation energy absorption primarily takes place in the upper atmosphere.
- We know from radio transmissions that ionization of the atmosphere varies considerably between day and night.

The blue sky appears to be the air molecules in the upper atmosphere being excited by the absorption of energy and emitting a very low level of blue light. Against the background of black Space, it appears to be a relatively uniform blue glow.

The following diagram shows the electromagnetic sky of day and night.

Light Forensics © Steven Magee

The Electromagnetic Sky

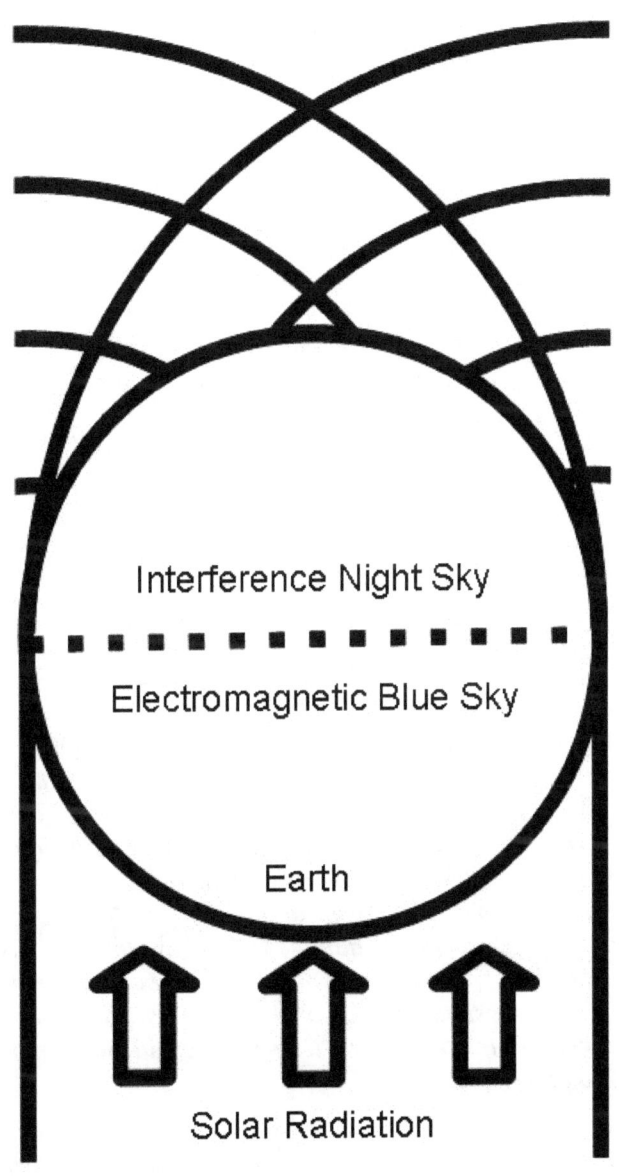

Light Forensics © Steven Magee

Wikipedia states the following about St. Elmo's Fire: *St. Elmo's fire is a mixture of gas and plasma, as are flames in general and stars. The electric field around the object in question causes ionization of the air molecules, producing a faint glow easily visible in low-light conditions. Approximately 1000 volts per centimeter induces St. Elmo's fire; however, this number is greatly dependent on the geometry of the object in question. Sharp points tend to require lower voltage levels to produce the same result because electric fields are more concentrated in areas of high curvature, thus discharges are more intense at the ends of pointed objects.*

Conditions that can generate St.Elmo's fire are present during thunderstorms, when high voltage levels are present between clouds and the ground underneath. Air molecules glow due to the effects of such voltage, producing St. Elmo's fire.

The nitrogen and oxygen in the Earth's atmosphere causes St. Elmo's fire to fluoresce with blue or violet light; this is similar to the mechanism that causes neon lights to glow.

Wikipedia states the following about the edge of Space: *The Kármán line lies at an altitude of 100 kilometres (62 mi) above the Earth's sea level, and is commonly used to define the boundary between the Earth's atmosphere and outer space. This definition is accepted by the Fédération Aéronautique Internationale (FAI), which is an international standard setting and record-keeping body for aeronautics and astronautics.*

The line was named after Theodore von Kármán, (1881– 1963) a Hungarian-American engineer and physicist who was active primarily in the fields of aeronautics and astronautics. He first calculated that around this altitude the Earth's atmosphere becomes too thin for aeronautical purposes (because any vehicle at this altitude would have to travel faster than orbital velocity in order to derive sufficient aerodynamic lift from the atmosphere to support itself). Also, there is an abrupt increase in atmospheric temperature and interaction with solar radiation.

Wikipedia states the following about the solar wind: *The solar wind is a stream of charged particles released from the upper atmosphere of the Sun. It mostly consists of electrons and protons with energies usually between 1.5 and 10 keV. The stream of particles varies in temperature and speed over time. These particles can escape the Sun's gravity because of their high kinetic energy and the high temperature of the corona.*

It would appear that the blue sky is actually produced by the solar wind and solar radiation exciting air molecules to emit light, just like a neon lamp!

The blue sky clearly turns off at sunset and starts again at sunrise. It also appears to turn off during an eclipse of the Sun by the Moon. During these times, great changes in the electromagnetic radiation environment are known to occur. Part of this change will come from the blue sky electromagnetic emissions that are created by the excited air molecules turning off.

I call this theory of electromagnetically excited air molecules that cause the sky to glow blue:

"Electromagnetic Blue Sky"

The next photograph shows the blue sky at the edge of Space.

"Staring at the blue sky causes insomnia to occur in the human"

Steven Magee

Light Forensics © Steven Magee

The blue sky glow at the edge of Space.

Light Forensics © Steven Magee

Nighttime

What is nighttime? One answer to this question that I have heard is that it is an absence of daylight. Having given it some thought and become aware of effects that are taking place in plants during the nighttime, I now know this not to be entirely correct.

Nighttime appears to be a heavily filtered and interference form of daytime. There is some daylight still present during the night, it is just that our human eyes are not able to detect it. Animals that have night vision have evolved with eyes that are able to function in this much lower level of light. Illumination by the stars becomes prevalent, each of which is a nuclear reactor. The cycles of the moon and planets come into play, as do comets and shooting stars.

On the way to nighttime we pass through the period known as sunset. This period marks a distinct change that lasts approximately two hours where great changes in the lighting levels and types of radiation occur. At sunset as the Sun is coming down to the horizon, the light becomes an interference type of light due to crossing the horizon and also by being heavily filtered by the atmosphere. The same effect happens at sunrise. Sunrise is different from sunset due to the air being cooler. As such, less interference and filtering effects take place during sunrise.

The next diagram shows the cycles of light over one day.

"There they stand, the innumerable stars, shining in order like a living hymn, written in light."

N.P. Willis

Light Forensics © Steven Magee

The Daily Cycles of Solar Radiation

Solar radiation levels are constantly changing during a day.

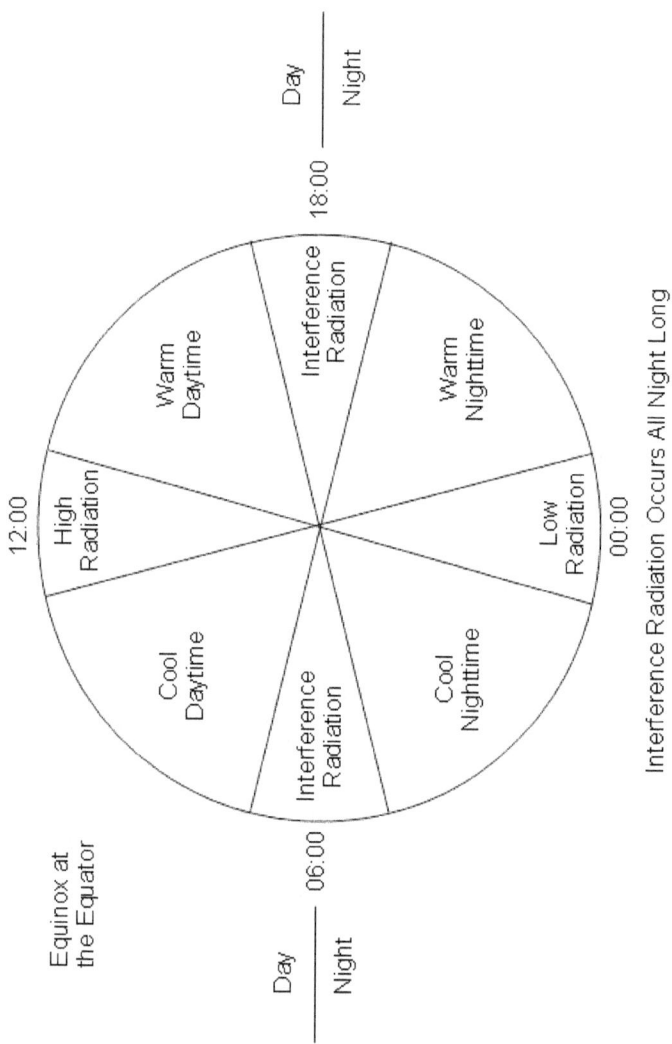

Aurora

If the sky glows blue in the daytime, then what is making it glow green of a nighttime at the poles?

The answer to that question is that there is a very dense set of magnetic field lines at the north and south poles that cannot be found anywhere else on the planet. It was established a long time ago that the auroras were generated by the solar wind and increased brightness coincided with solar flare activity. Solar flares eject massive amounts of energy and particles into the solar system. These waves of gas and energy vigorously interact with the dense magnetic field lines of the Earth's poles and excite the atmosphere to emit light.

The light generated is not blue like the blue sky. The blue sky is generated by radiation absorption from the Sun and solar wind. This aurora light is generated by energy and particle flows through a dense magnetic field and atmosphere and is a very different process of light generation. The aurora appears to be a round shape on the Earth due to the energy particles from the solar wind following the magnetic lines into the Earth.

The Aurora are predominantly green. However, they are also seen to glow blue and red. The electrical lighting industry established that it could make gases change color depending on the level of vacuum and type of energy stimulation that they received. One gas can be made to emit different colors by varying the specific conditions that cause it to emit light. The same processes appear to be occurring at the poles.

Components of the solar wind are helium and hydrogen. Helium is known for its many colors and the electrical lighting industry has demonstrated its ability to glow green. The helium content of the solar wind greatly increases during solar flares. They meet the air of the Earth as they interact with the magnetic fields of the poles.

The known colors of glowing gasses involved with the aurora are:

- Air: Purple to blue.
- Helium: White to orange; under some conditions may be gray, blue, or green-blue.
- Hydrogen: Lavender at low currents, pink to magenta over 10 milliamps.

Anytime that you look up to the clear sky and see colors in it, you should be suspecting that you are looking at a flow of energy through the sky that is causing a gas to glow. The blue sky glow is so bright that we can only see the moon and planets through it during the daytime. The Aurora is much dimmer and we can see the stars through it. This indicates that the electromagnetic energy flows associated with the Aurora are far less than what creates the blue sky. The Aurora can get very bright during solar flares that hit Earth.

You can see the Aurora in the next picture.

"Earth and sky...are excellent school masters and teach some of us more than we can ever learn from books"

John Lubbock

Light Forensics © Steven Magee

South Pole Green Auroa

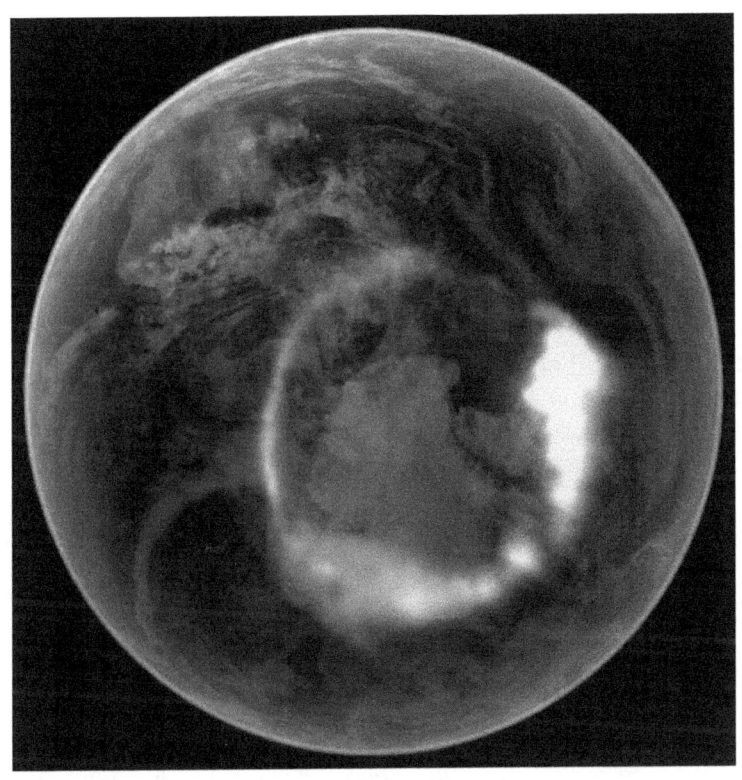

Light Forensics © Steven Magee

Moonlight

Can moonlight affect your health? History says it can. The word "lunatic" is developed from the word "lune", which means Moon.

It appears that in the past, some people would go crazy if they were exposed to moonlight. This is documented as happening when someone would sleep in view of the Moon.

The Moon has a lighting level that is only 1/500,000 of the Sun. A full moon has a lighting level of just 0.3 lux! However, this reflected sunlight that the Moon creates is modified by the surface of the Moon and may be toxic to humans. There is a reason why the full Moon is associated with strange events!

The color temperature of the Moon is cooler than that of the Sun and therefore its light is very different from the Sun. The Moon emits a non-parallel form of light, also known as scattered light.

"For 50 years, nuclear power stations have produced three products which only a lunatic could want: bomb-explosive plutonium, lethal radioactive waste and electricity so dear it has to be heavily subsidized. They leave to future generations the task, and most of the cost, of making safe sites that have been polluted half-way to eternity."

James Buchan

Starlight

Starlight comes from the largest nuclear reactors that we know of! Every star is a giant ball of nuclear energy that is burning at rates that are so vast that they are hard to comprehend. When it goes dark and the stars come out, we get subjected to the radiation from the stars. They illuminate the nighttime.

Starlight is an essential requirement for the human to be exposed to. We have developed in harmony with them. However, there is a type of star that we know can make humans sick. These are called supernovas. Supernovas occur when stars explode and create a bright glowing star in the sky.

The supernova star emits a large amount of radiation in a very short period of time. If one were to explode near to us, then it could cause a mass extinction due to the greatly increased radiation levels! This effect is very well known in astronomy.

It has long been speculated that the Star of Bethlehem may have been a supernova that occurred at that time.

"Dear brightest star o'er Bethlehem, O let your precious light shine in with hope and peace toward men in every home tonight."

Swedish Carol

Comets

Comets have shown us what the solar wind does to objects in Space. The long tail extending out from the comet is the solar wind blowing particles from the object off into Space. In the case of comets it is solids, liquids, and gas that are blown away by the solar wind and the solar radiation effects.

A similar tail follows the Earth. However, the Earth's tail cannot be observed, due to the protective atmosphere. There are particles being blown off the Earth as in the comets, just much less of them. What we have is an invisible tail of solar wind particles on the dark side of the Earth.

The important concept of the solar wind is that Space is not empty. It is an energy and particle filled environment that interacts with whatever is in it! Astronomers call this "Dark Energy".

The radiation that is emitted by comets has long been associated with historical events. They were regarded as harbingers of doom throughout history. Given that they do change the ground level radiation, it is reasonable to assume that this is a correct observation that they can be toxic to life on Earth.

A comet can be seen in the next picture.

"(Only by) the good influence of our conduct may we bring salvation in human affairs; or like a fatal comet we may bring destruction in our train"

Desiderius Erasmus

Light Forensics © Steven Magee

The comet's tail always points away from the Sun due to the solar wind.

Light Forensics © Steven Magee

Solar Radiation & Weather

The strength of the Sun at ground level is dependent on the weather. The main factors that affect the Sun's strength are clouds, snow, shade and latitude. Let us now explore the effects of the weather in more detail:

Irradiance

Irradiance is a measure of how much sunlight the Sun is producing at ground level. It is given in watts per meter squared or W/m^2. This value can range from $0W/m^2$ at night through to over $1,500W/m^2$ during a day interspersed with large fluffy clouds. This value of $1,500W/m^2$ is larger than what you would receive in Space. The reason why we can get greater values at ground level is due to what is known as the "Cloud Effect". Normally the sunlight is traveling in a straight line from the Sun to the ground with some atmospheric scattering. However, when clouds are present they can also reflect and can act like lenses to send some extra sunlight to the ground. This effect can be a few minutes long in duration when it occurs. The diagrams on the following pages demonstrates solar radiation "Cloud Effect".

Reflected Cloud Effect

The sunlight bounces off the clouds and is lensed into a high powered area of radiation.

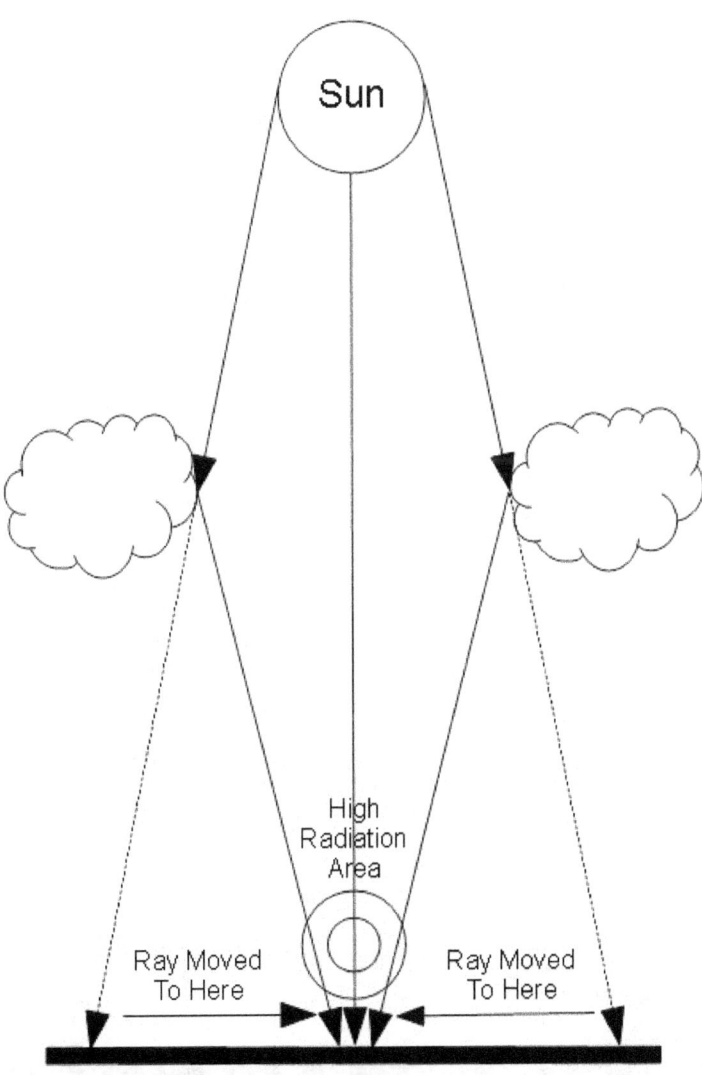

Light Forensics © Steven Magee

Refraction Cloud Effect

The weight of the cloud depresses the boundary layer to cause lensing of the solar radiation.

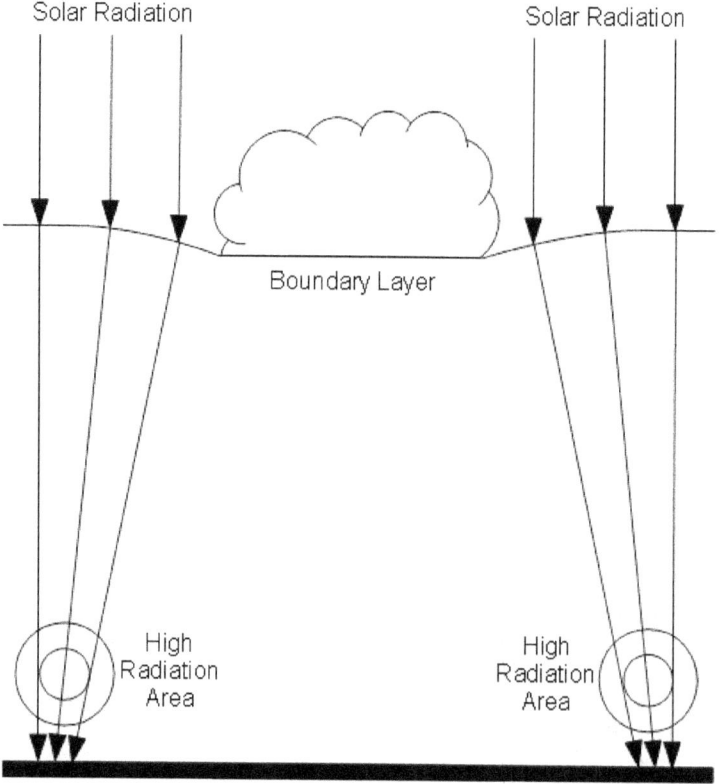

Light Forensics © Steven Magee

Other effects on irradiance are the snow effect, the water effect (lake/ocean/wet surfaces after rain), the building effect and albedo. Snow cover, water, glass covered buildings, reflective painted buildings and roofs, and the albedo of the area surrounding the human environment can reflect extra sunlight into it. Each effect can produce an increase in power. If you find yourself having to wear sunglasses in your environment for your eyes to be comfortable, then you probably have light reflections taking place.

Air Mass

Air mass is a measurement of the amount of atmosphere that the sunlight has to pass through to get to the ground. It varies with the seasons and also the location on the Earth. Within the tropics, air mass will reach its maximum power value of 1 during summertime. Air mass 1 corresponds to the Sun being directly overhead, air mass increases as the Sun moves from directly overhead down to the horizon. At the horizon the air mass is approximately 38.

Locations that are at or near air mass 1 in summertime in the USA are all Hawaiian islands, Florida and Texas. In summertime the air mass will move closer to 1 in the continental USA.

Clouds

Clouds come in many forms. An important question is how do clouds affect solar irradiance? The list below will help with understanding the effects of clouds on solar irradiance at air mass 1 (solar noon within the tropics in summertime):

- Clear, sunny skies will give approximately $1,130 W/m^2$. The transmission characteristics of the atmosphere will vary in clear skies, sometimes being relatively transparent and other times being more opaque and this affects irradiance values. Air quality is a major factor for the transmission of sunlight through the atmosphere. Particulate matter in the atmosphere will reduce the transmission level and may cause interference effects.

- Thin cirrus will give approximately $1,000 W/m^2$. Thin cirrus will give even and relatively stable irradiance levels due to scattering of the light.
- Thick cirrus will give approximately $750 W/m^2$.
- Thin clouds will give about $500 W/m^2$.
- Thick clouds will give about $250 W/m^2$. No shadows on the ground will be present.
- Thick clouds with a visibly dark sky will give about $100 W/m^2$. No shadows on the ground will be present. You will not be able to see the location of the Sun in the sky.
- Broken clouds will give surges of about $1,500 W/m^2$ and reductions to about $100 W/m^2$ of irradiance due to the cloud effect. The rate and length of time for these surges and reductions is dependent on the speed of the clouds passing in front of the Sun. They highly modulate the sunlight power levels.

Shade

Shade significantly reduces the solar radiation levels in the human environment. The best form of shade is that from nature, such as trees. The optimum solar radiation environment for the human is under the tree canopy in the shade.

Light Forensics © Steven Magee

Altitude

A higher altitude location will increase the amount of solar radiation in the human environment, due to less scattering and absorption of the sunlight by the atmosphere. It also acts as a natural cooler. Generally a high altitude location will have a higher percentage of clearer skies during a year.

Snow and Ice

The reflections from the snow and ice will increase the solar radiation in wintertime. The highest annual solar radiation power levels may occur in this environment.

Seasons

We have four distinct seasons of winter, spring, summer and autumn. We can word this another way as winter solstice (December 21), spring equinox (March 20), summer solstice (June 21) and autumn equinox (September 22). What does this mean to solar radiation power levels?

- The length of the day.
- The angle of the Sun (air mass).
- Heating and cooling.
- Foliage.
- Clouds.
- Rain.
- Hail.
- Snow.
- Albedo.

Winter solstice is the shortest day of the year and summer solstice is the longest day of the year. Spring and autumn equinoxes are when daytime is the same length of time as nighttime.

Regarding the angle of the Sun in the USA, winter solstice is when the Sun is at the lowest in the sky, or 23.5 degrees below the equator and summer solstice is when it is 23.5 degrees above the equator. Spring and autumn equinoxes are when the Sun is directly overhead at solar noon at the equator.

The changing seasons will affect rainfall and rain will cause the albedo to change during the year. A barren snow covered field will be a lot different to one filled with corn or flowers.

Climate Change

The Earth's weather system is highly complicated and we struggle to predict how it will behave. Massive localized flooding has started to become commonplace in human society. Historic weather records are commonly being broken. It's not just high temperatures, but seasonal snow patterns, cold weather temperatures and strange changes in the seasons. The glaciers are receding and the ice caps at the poles are melting at alarming rates.

Changing the composition of the atmospheric gasses is a strong possibility for causing these changes.

It is a scary thought that we are adding large amounts of trapped exhaust gasses into the air that we breathe through the use of fossil fuels and industrial processes. The biomass that created the gas, coal and oil may have developed in a different atmosphere and may have had a different gas composition to the atmosphere that developed in harmony with the humans. Adding these previously trapped exhaust gasses into our current atmosphere may be like pouring poison into the human air supply.

Climate change is very real and poses an extremely serious threat to mankind.

The book "The Weather of the Future: Heat Waves, Extreme Storms, and Other Scenes from a Climate-Changed Planet" by Heidi Cullen gives an insight of what could be heading our way.

"We are playing Russian roulette with features of the planet's atmosphere that will profoundly impact generations to come. How long are we willing to gamble?"

David Suzuki

Light Forensics © Steven Magee

High Cirrus

High cirrus may be a relatively new phenomenon. Old paintings of high cirrus do not seem to be prevalent. It is a common view in the sky today. High cirrus may be a result of the following:

- Development of industry.
- Development of cars.
- Development of air travel.
- Development of refrigeration and air conditioning.
- Development and use of chemicals.
- The massive release of trapped water vapor into the atmosphere.
- The massive release of previously trapped gasses into the atmosphere.

Increased water vapor in the atmosphere appears to be causing solar radiation lensing, filtering, polarization, diffraction and interference effects. It is highly undesirable and the long term effects of this are currently unknown.

If high cirrus is a modern development, then we have to ask ourselves how serious is this? Research into ground based solar radiation indicates that high cirrus raises the ground based solar radiation levels at times. High levels of solar radiation may be able to induce disease into the human body.

This is a major problem for ground level solar radiation. It may be linked in the future to killing off some of the coral reefs in the oceans and possibly making some species of plants and animals head towards extinction. The human race may already be heading down this route as well.

Light Forensics © Steven Magee

Fish and whales are being reported to have sunburn in large numbers. Coral reefs, commonly referred to as the forests of the sea, are dying off all over the world. Is the lensing effect of the clouds causing this to occur?

High cirrus appears to have an effect on light that is similar to fiber optics. As it passes in front of the Sun, it appears to channel the sunlight through it. All of the cirrus near to the Sun lights up with the light passing through it.

"Clouds come floating into my life, no longer to carry rain or usher storm, but to add color to my sunset sky."

Rabindranath Tagore

Light Forensics © Steven Magee

Water Vapor Lensing of Solar Radiation

The sunlight has smeared into the vapor and produced a rainbow.

Thin Cirrus Lens

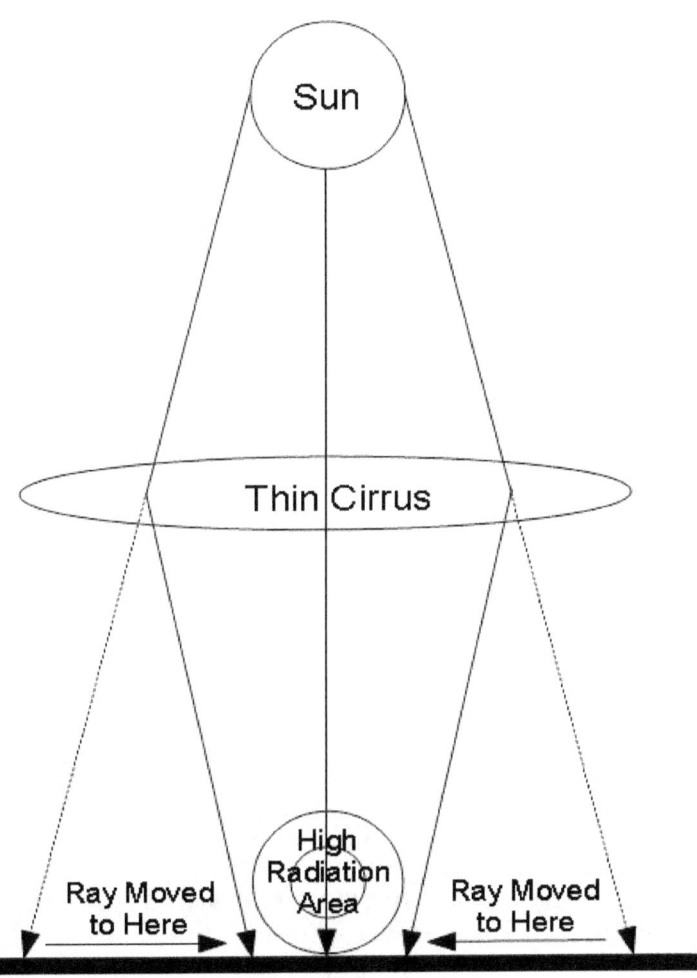

Chemtrail Light

Aircraft chemtrails (contrails) are one of the newest phenomenon's of mankind. High altitude jet aircraft leave tails of hot white compressed engine exhaust gasses behind them. These trails can linger for hours and look like scars in the blue sky. They eclipse the Sun, cast shadows and change the ground level radiation environment.

Many people have associated them with strange health effects that occur in populations who live in areas that these trails appear above. It is likely only a matter of time before we see the conditions that these people report become known as "Chemtrail Sickness" in the medical field. The sickness symptoms appear to be diverse that these people report.

Chemtrails cause filtering, diffraction, interference, and polarization effects on the solar radiation that passes through them. You would expect them to affect the populations that they occur over as they are changing the environmental conditions below. The human has not evolved with chemtrails and has no genetic adaptation to them.

The chemtrails are deposited into the jet streams in the atmosphere. The jet streams are massive high altitude air currents that flow around the world. No one really knows what these do to the atmosphere or what the long term implications are to the Earth and the life on it.

"The jet stream is the controlling influence over the world's weather systems."
Michael Fish

Light Forensics © Steven Magee

Aircraft Chemical Trails

The Sun as viewed entering a jet aircraft chemical trail. Chemical trails of all types may cause toxic light.

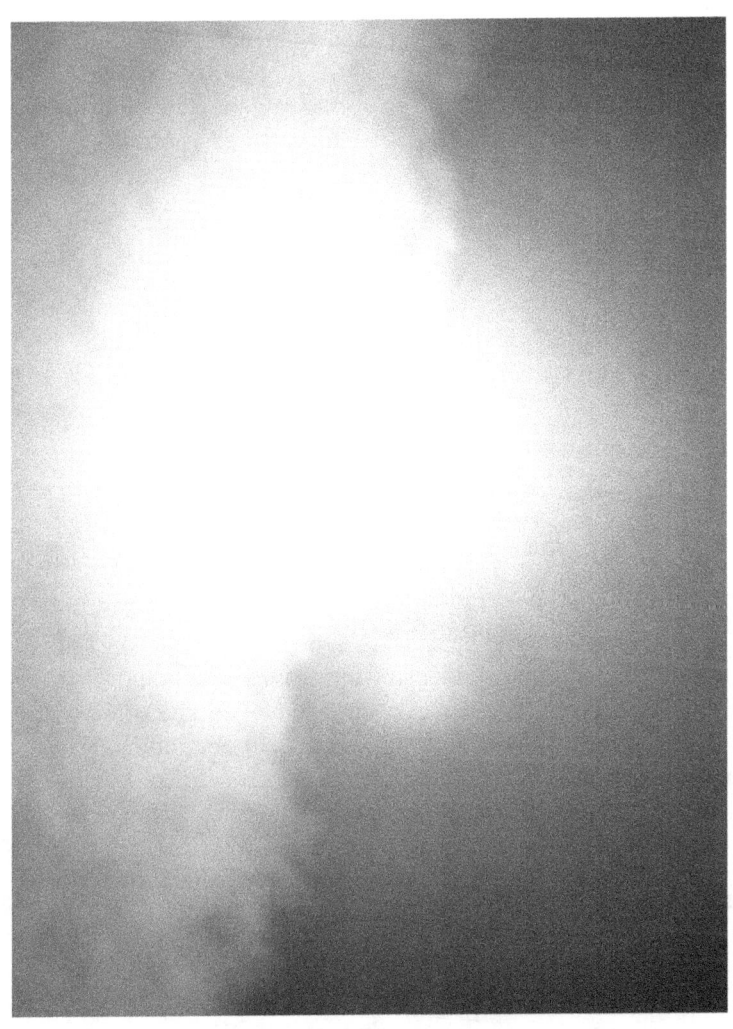

Light Forensics © Steven Magee

Earthquake Light

Earthquake light is being reported around the world. Earthquake light seems to precede large earthquakes in the world. It appears as rainbow effects in the clouds and many people report strange cloud formations. What could be causing this effect to occur?

First, we need to understand what sunlight is. Sunlight is solar radiation that originated at the largest nuclear reactor in the solar system, called the Sun. Solar radiation contains many types of frequencies of radiation and is classed as broad spectrum radiation. Solar radiation is energy.

There are a number of things that are definite about the atmosphere:

- It is polluted.
- The pollution is acting like a filter.
- There are many more molecules in it.
- The solar radiation transmission has changed.
- The clouds have changed.

So what could be causing vivid colors in the sky? It is most likely pollution condensing out from gas to liquid form in the atmosphere. Have you ever noticed that oil and water when mixed together makes color effects like that of rainbows? It appears that air and pollution may do the same trick. Vivid colors are characteristic of the light interference effects that fossil fuels can produce. These vivid colored clouds are called "Rainbow Clouds". They are also associated with clouds that have ice crystals in them.

So what about the earthquake effects? Could these be true? Perhaps. Solar radiation has an energy content of 1,366

W/m² in Space. So to get the next concept you need to adjust your thinking to that of energy. The earthquake effect is associated with strange colors in the sky. This appears to be a result of interference.

Interferometry is the study of light interference. Now, we know that solar radiation is energy and that the energy waves are interfering with each other. This produces what is known as constructive and deconstructive interference. So the pollution is causing energy interference, so it may produce radio waves, right? And it appears that it does, low frequency radio waves between 10 kHz and 20kHz are commonly reported at the same time of the observations of earthquake light.

So how much energy interference could it produce? It's hard to say, but large scale interference over an area of 10 square kilometers could produce up to 13.66 gigawatts of energy interference if all of the energy was converted!

$$10 km^2 \times 1,000,000 m^2 \times 1,366 W/m^2 = 13,660,000,000 W$$

An area of 10,000 square kilometers could potentially produce 13.66 terawatts of energy interference!

$$10,000 km^2 \times 1,000,000 m^2 \times 1,366 W/m^2 = 13,660,000,000,000 W$$

Most power stations are producing about 1 gigawatt of energy. That makes this equivalent to 13,660 power stations of energy production. It is a lot of energy!

So where is all of the energy going to go? Probably into the core of the Earth. Unfortunately, on its way there it will pass through the human environment and it is currently unknown if this presents a problem to the core or to the surface environment and the life there.

Earthquake light is an unproven, but currently plausible, effect in nature.

Light Forensics © Steven Magee

The theory presented here is known as the "Atmospheric Energy Interference" effect.

Examples of possible earthquake light are shown in the following images.

"An earthquake achieves what the law promises but does not in practice maintain - the equality of all men"

Ignazio Silon

Light Forensics © Steven Magee

Possible Interference Cloud Formation

Holes in the clouds may cause interference effects.

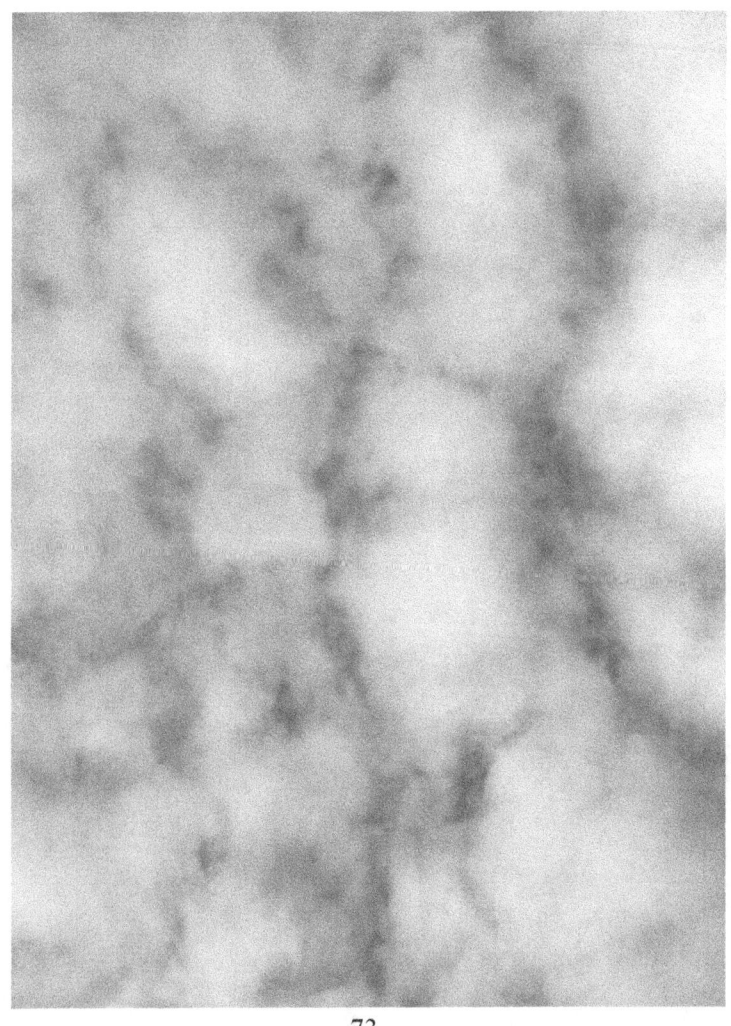

Light Forensics © Steven Magee

Colors in Clouds

Colors in clouds may be interference effects.

Volcanic Light

Filtering the light with pollution is well known to affect nature and human health. We have extensive knowledge of this effect from volcanic eruptions. One of the most notable effects was observed during the 1783 eruption of the Laki volcano in Iceland. This eruption filled the skies of Europe and North America with volcanic smog.

The eruption brought strange weather patterns, hail, and thunderstorms to these areas. The atmosphere would have been filled with gases and particles from the eruption. The crops failed and livestock died. There was a massive famine in the human population and strange health conditions showed up. The Sun was reported to look either very pale or blood red during that period. The summer in the UK was hot and the winter was severely cold. Extensive reports of fog are recorded during this period.

Gilbert White recorded his perceptions of the Sun at Selborne, Hampshire, England: *The sun, at noon, looked as blank as a clouded moon, and shed a rust-coloured ferruginous light on the ground, and floors of rooms; but was particularly lurid and blood-coloured at rising and setting.*

A volcanic red sunset can be seen in the following picture that was taken through the volcanic smog in Hawaii. People that I know on the island of Hawaii commonly report that their health improves when they are away on vacation or business trips. It is likely due to detoxing from effects of the volcanic smog.

Light Forensics © Steven Magee

The Red Volcanic Smog Sunset

Volcanic smog creates red sunsets due to filtering.

Light Forensics © Steven Magee

Benjamin Franklin documents the fog in the USA in a 1784 lecture: *During several of the summer months of the year 1783, when the effect of the Sun's rays to heat the Earth in these northern regions should have been greater, there existed a constant fog over all Europe, and a great part of North America. This fog was of a permanent nature; it was dry, and the rays of the Sun seemed to have little effect towards dissipating it, as they easily do a moist fog, arising from water.*

It is interesting to note that during experiments performed at Nikola Tesla's Colorado laboratory, he reports generating fog with certain electrical frequencies of energy. He states: ***"In Colorado I succeeded one day in precipitating a dense fog. There was a mist outside, but when I turned on the current the cloud in the laboratory became so dense that when the hand was held only a few inches from the face it could not be seen."***

This persistent fog was most likely produced by atmospheric energy interference.

There were two periods of high mortality in the UK and these were August-September 1783 and January-February 1784. During these periods approximately 20,000 extra deaths occurred. Diseases of the gastrointestinal tract were widely reported as being the cause of death in many cases. The deaths appeared to be in people who worked in outdoor occupations.

Volcanic smog is similar in nature to earthquake light. It causes atmospheric energy interference to occur. We know from NASA research that the gastrointestinal tract is affected by radiation exposure. It is likely that the volcanic smog caused atmospheric energy interference to occur which severely affected the population where it was present. The unnatural electromagnetic environment would have caused some very weird health conditions to show up in the people who were exposed to it.

Regarding volcanic emissions, the CDC states: *Exposure to ash can be harmful. Infants, elderly people, and people with respiratory conditions such as asthma, emphysema, and other chronic lung diseases may have problems if they* breathe in volcanic ash. *Ash is gritty, abrasive, sometimes corrosive, and always unpleasant. Small ash particles can abrade (scratch) the front of the eye. Ash particles may contain crystalline silica, a material that causes a respiratory disease called silicosis.*

Most gases from a volcano quickly blow away. However, heavy gases such as carbon dioxide and hydrogen sulfide can collect in low-lying areas. The most common volcanic gas is water vapor, followed by carbon dioxide and sulfur dioxide. Sulfur dioxide can cause breathing problems in both healthy people and people with asthma and other respiratory problems. Other volcanic gases include hydrogen chloride, carbon monoxide, and hydrogen fluoride. Amounts of these gases vary widely from one volcanic eruption to the next.

Although gases usually blow away rapidly, it is possible that people who are close to the volcano or who are in the low-lying areas downwind may be exposed to levels that may affect health. At low levels, gases can irritate the eyes, nose, and throat. At higher levels, gases can cause rapid breathing, headache, dizziness, swelling and spasm of the throat, and suffocation.

On the island of Hawaii, the following problems are reported during periods of high volcanic smog (vog):

- Headache.
- Itchy eyes.
- Watery eyes.
- Congested sinuses.
- Breathing problems.
- Asthma attack.
- Feeling of pressure on the chest.
- Bronchitis.
- Prickly sensation.

Light Forensics © Steven Magee

- Low energy.
- Desire to sleep.

Extended vog exposure may lead to:

- Degraded lung function.
- Compromised immune system.
- Filtered sunlight related health problems (toxic light).
- Systemic poisoning.
- Poor mental and physical health.
- Multiple Chemical Sensitivity (MCS).

The worst pollution from Hawaii vog is noted to occur near to the inversion layer at approximately 7,400 feet (2,225 meters). The air quality gets better both above and below that altitude. High altitude air and sea level air are reported as having the best air quality, although the sea level air can still be heavily contaminated by the vog.

"Red sky at night, sailors delight; red sky at morning, sailors warning"

Proverb

Water Light

Pollution water films are a problem as they will generate water light interference. Any water life forms that are being subjected to filtered, polarized, diffraction and interference light may not develop correctly. It has been noticed around the world that the frogs are having significant development problems and pollution water films may be causing some of these issues.

Plastics are accumulating in the ocean and there are large groupings of them occurring around the world. The marine life consumes these plastics and quite often dies from the effects of ingesting foreign materials that their digestive system cannot process. The optical effects that plastics create by floating on the surface of the water are likely to be harmful to the marine life below.

The water film interference light ray diagram is shown on the next page. The following page shows the rainbow colors that interference light can sometimes generate.

"Water is the driving force of all nature."
Leonardo da Vinci

Oil Film Light Ray Diagram

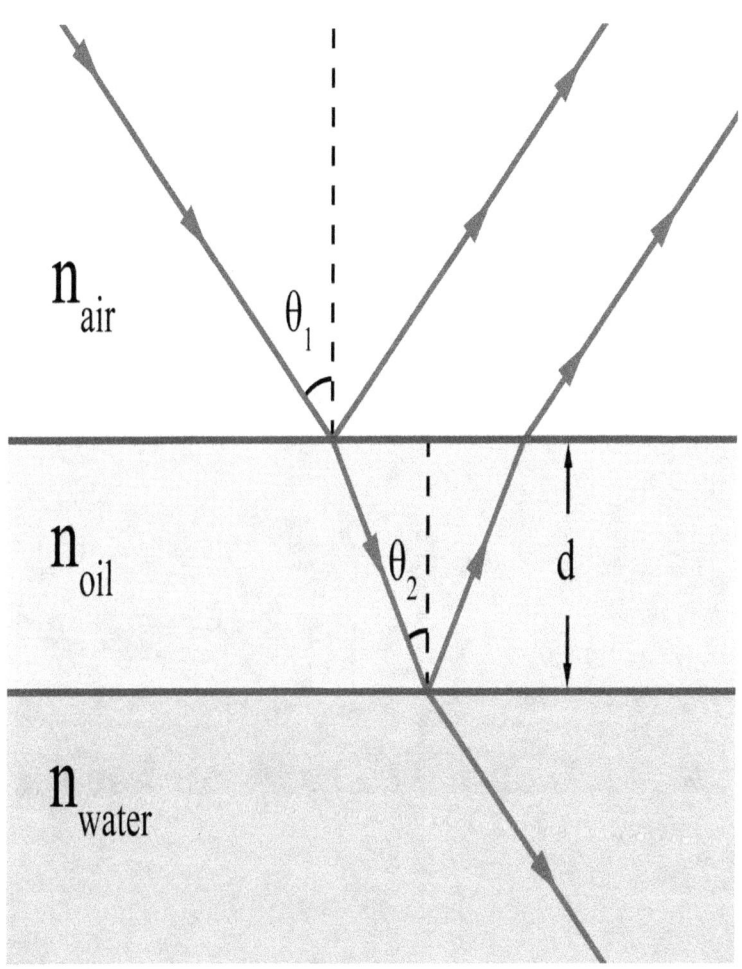

Oil Film Interference Colors

The oil film floating on top of the water has created a rainbow of colors.

Light Forensics © Steven Magee

Turbulent Light

Turbulence can cause lensing. Many things can cause turbulence to occur:

- Smoke.
- Heat.
- Solar power systems.
- Open areas.
- Wind.
- Structures.
- Wind turbines.

Once turbulence has been set up, solar radiation lensing may occur. This is commonly seen as distant objects shimmering. This is shown on the following pages.

"When a system is in turbulence, the turbulence is not just out there in the environment, but is a part of the organization or organism that you are looking at."
Kevin Kelly

Light Forensics © Steven Magee

Structure Turbulence

The turbulence from structures may set up lensing of solar radiation.

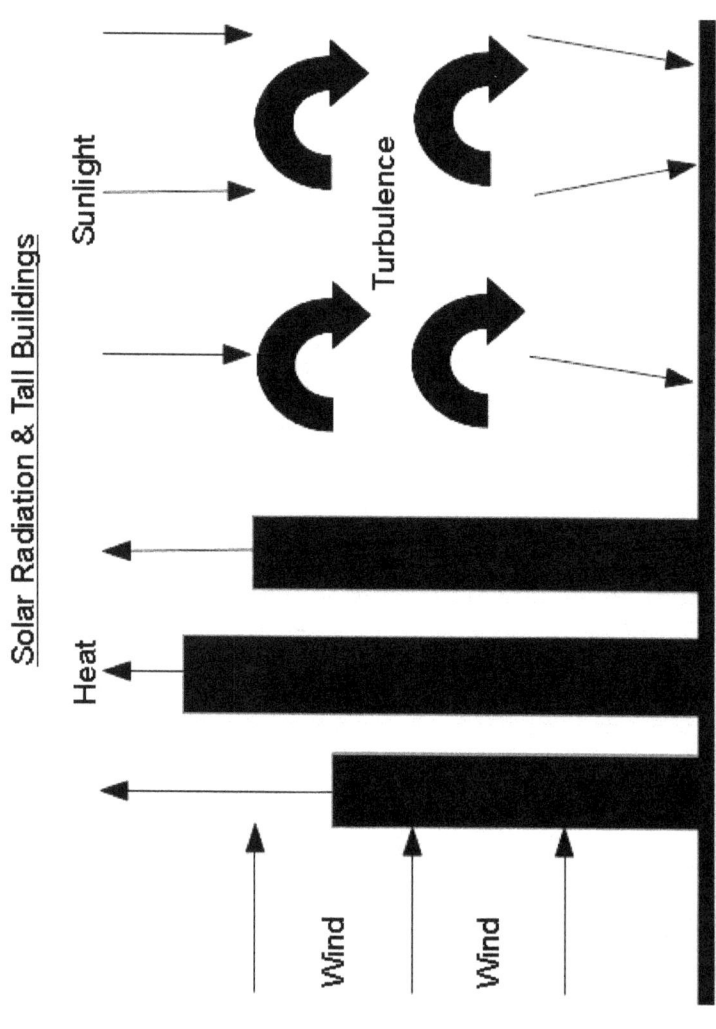

Hot Air & Smoke

Heat haze from smoke or hot air may set up turbulent air flows that cause lensing effects to occur.

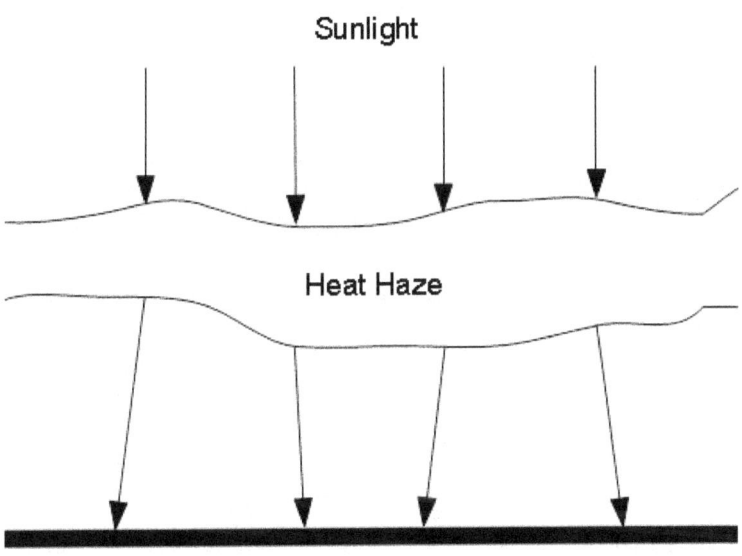

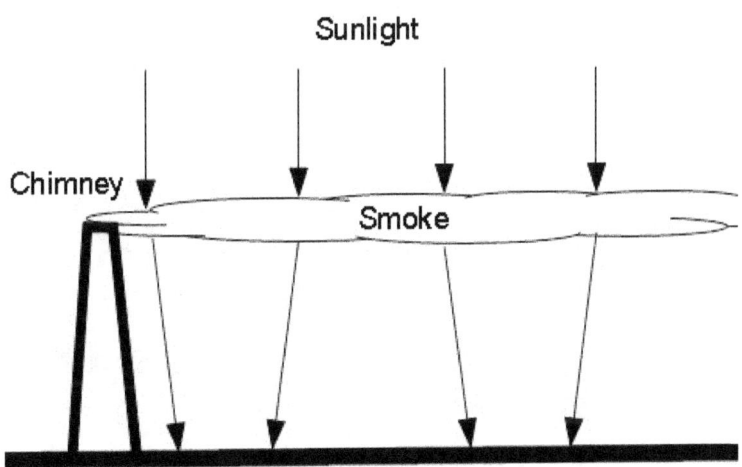

Light Forensics © Steven Magee

Reflected Light

Albedo is the Siamese twin of the cloud effect. They go everywhere together. Make sure that you are considering both effects when estimating solar radiation power levels. Albedo is the reflectivity of surfaces. A very well known effect in the world of astronomy.

Everything reflects light, even matt black surfaces reflect some low level of light, that is how we can see it. Everything our eyes can see is created from reflected light from surfaces. If your eyes can see these things, so can the rest of your body. If you need to put on your sunglasses, think about the reflection effects that may cause your eyes to be uncomfortable. Your body will sense the increase of solar radiation power levels as heat and you may start to sweat as your body warms up. You will need to identify these effects as it may be able to impact your health.

You should get used to assessing your environment for these albedo effects and start to avoid them if possible. Nature suppresses solar radiation for a reason. These albedo effects will probably put your body into an environment that it was never designed to cope with and the long term effects may be undesirable. The short term effect will be sunburn and possibly heatstroke.

Here is a list from Wikipedia that shows the albedo in various objects:

Object	Albedo
Fresh asphalt	0.04
Worn asphalt	0.12
Conifer forest	0.08 to 0.15
Deciduous trees	0.15 to 0.18
Bare soil	0.17
Green grass	0.25
Desert sand	0.4
New concrete	0.55
Ocean Ice	0.5–0.7
Fresh snow	0.80–0.90

It is important to realize that reflected light is polarized light. It is different from direct sunlight even though the human eye cannot sense that difference. There are many animals in nature that are sensitive to polarized light and polarized light may have some effects on the human that we have yet to discover.

In the next diagram we can see some situations that create the albedo effect.

"There are two kinds of light - the glow that illumines, and the glare that obscures."
James Thurber

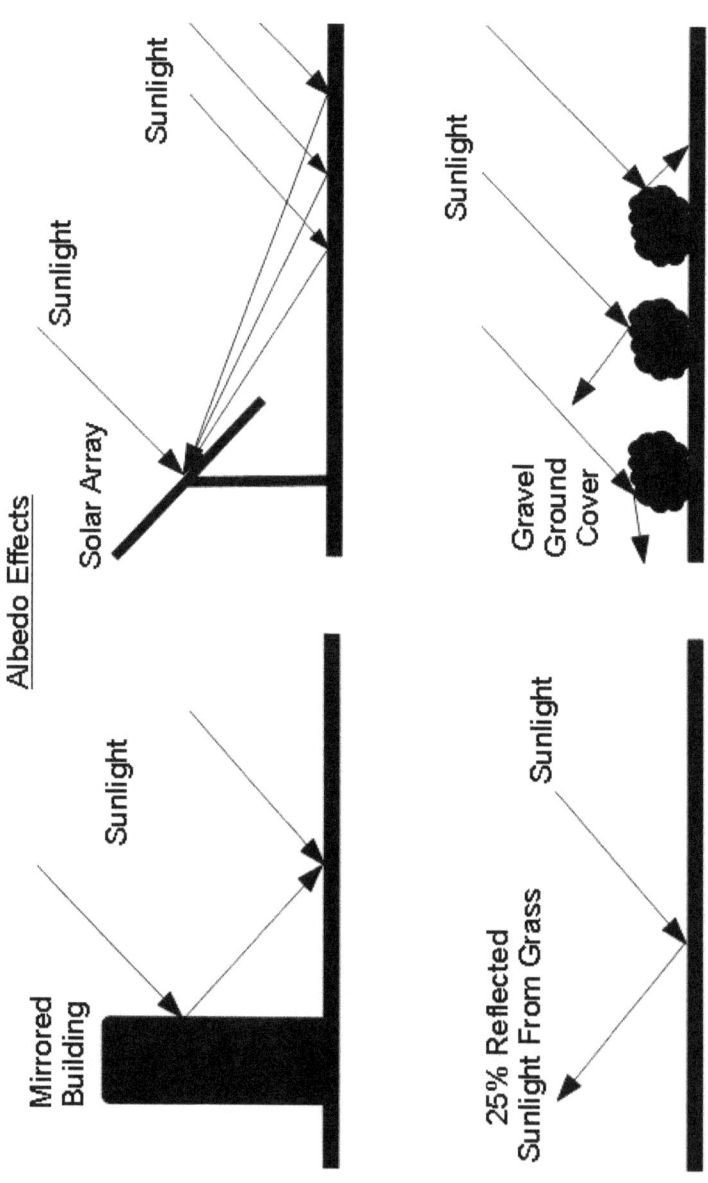

Light Forensics © Steven Magee

High Solar Radiation

We are constantly walking around in an energy field of broad spectrum solar radiation that originated at the largest nuclear reactor in the solar system, called the Sun. It is important that this energy level be kept low for human health. The trees and plants, also known as nature, provide this function and aid human health.

You should avoid watching the sunrises and sunsets regularly due to the filtered nature of the solar radiation. It is this filtering that generates the amazing colors. Unfortunately, staring at the Sun during this time appears to be bad for human health. It may have the potential to make you ill through solar radiation induced disease if it becomes a regular habit.

General exposure to the direct view of the Sun delivers a lot of energy to your body and this can be felt as heat and also sensed by the eyes as brightness and you will need to wear sunglasses due to this. There are no doubts that the Sun is a carcinogen and it is wise to avoid direct views of it.

Glass rooms, such as conservatories, should be avoided. They are generally full of reflections and these boost the radiation levels inside them. If you have one of these rooms, you would be wise to fill it with plant life in order to reduce the solar radiation levels inside it.

East, South and West facing windows let in a lot of direct solar radiation. You should not spend time too close to windows in this orientation. Natural window coverings are recommended. Plants should be placed next to windows like this. Desks should not be placed under these windows.

As for your eyes, ultraviolet (UV) rated sunglasses should be worn when the solar radiation levels are unnaturally high and these should be of an appropriate level of black tint. Mirrored, colored or polarized lenses should be avoided due to the modification of the solar radiation that takes place with these. You should view the light that your eyes receive as a nutrient and you want to keep it as natural as possible. Excessive solar radiation exposure in the human leads to radiation poisoning.

> *"It is with words as with sunbeams - the more they are condensed, the deeper they burn."*
> *Robert Southey*

Tree Light

Trees are made predominantly from air. The tree absorbs the air as it grows and converts it into a solid. The air is converted into wood and leaves. Trees trap large amounts of carbon through this process. It only occurs during the growth process.

Trees are composed of approximately 50% carbon and 50% water. This is where their mass comes from. Trees extract carbon from the air for their growth. The carbon dioxide levels in the atmosphere go down during spring and summer as the carbon is extracted for leaf growth. In autumn and winter it increases again as the trees drop the leaves and they are broken down through composting.

Modern human society has cut down a significant number of trees to allow the land to be farmed for agriculture use. The removal of these trees released the trapped carbon and water back into the environment and may have changed the atmospheric water and carbon content of the planet.

Have you noticed that new growth on trees is a much lighter green than the full grown leaves and stems? This appears to be due to a higher level of reflectivity of the new shoots. It appears that young growth on trees needs to absorb less solar radiation for a reason. It is quite possible that new growth would be damaged if it was absorbing the same levels of radiation as the older growth.

The tree canopy has many holes in it that the leaves create. In optics, the process of passing light through many apertures is called diffraction and interference. The light that is passing through the tree canopy is actually diffraction and interference light underneath it. It comprises of spreading light waves from each of the apertures. When interference light is photographed, it will show up as rings or an interference pattern.

Trees absorb the majority of solar radiation that hits them. In environments where the trees have been removed, the solar radiation levels at ground level generally have increased. This will result in increased heating of the ground and the surrounding air. It should come as no surprise that historic high temperature records appear to keep on being broken and it seems to be as a result of this.

The increased reflectivity of the ground means that more of the Sun's energy is lost by being reflected back into Space. This should produce a net loss of energy received from the Sun by the Earth when compared to the past. A hotter ground-level environment, higher ground-level solar radiation, and higher air temperatures with lower energy absorption by the Earth appears to be the result currently.

Trees are a very efficient solar radiation absorber and humans would be foolish to ignore the effect of global tree reduction on the Earth's environment. Their conversion of solar radiation into different forms of energy appears to be needed to keep the environment in balance. They also appear to maintain a healthy solar radiation environment for humans. It is also important in other organisms, such as fungi. Too much blue light kills fungi, so many types will not grow when there is a direct view of the blue sky.

Without the tree canopy reducing and modifying the solar radiation, humans are subjected to flicker. This is an effect that is happening at sub-second speeds that is not noticed by the human eye. However, a high speed camera that shoots several frames per second can see this occurring. The Sun is basically increasing and decreasing its intensity due to atmospheric distortions and interference. Astronomers know this affect as "Astronomical Seeing". This effect may be able to induce dizziness, fatigue, headaches, epilepsy and nausea. Modern flicker may be a consequence of atmospheric pollution and may be far more severe than in the past.

An effect that is similar to this is broken clouds passing in front of the Sun. These produce extreme power cycles in the solar radiation levels The power levels can change by over 90% very quickly. The human body appears to have problems with this high level of frequent power cycling and again may experience dizziness, fatigue, headaches, epilepsy, and nausea.

Solar radiation is made up of direct, diffuse, and albedo radiation power levels. Direct is the view of the Sun's disk, diffuse is the sky in general (the blue and cloudy part), and albedo is the reflections. Of these, direct contains over 90% of the energy and diffuse contains under 10%. There is no limit on the level that the reflections can be at and in a modern environment, such as a city, the albedo can increase the power levels many times of the sky based solar radiation of direct and diffuse combined. The trees prevent the albedo reflections from occurring.

Trees appear to have a major function in the regulation of the global environment. Most people relate trees to the regulation of gasses in the atmosphere. Trees also appear to have a major function in the regulation of solar radiation absorption and water absorption by the Earth and this aspect of trees requires further study.

So why did we cut them down and pave our human environment with man-made materials? I'm really not sure, you will have to ask the architects and city planners that question. It appears to have been a mistake.

To sum up, trees are known to provide the following functions:

- Trap carbon through growth.
- Absorb almost all solar radiation.
- Convert a small amount of solar radiation to a different broad spectrum of scattered solar radiation.
- Prevent solar radiation reflections.
- Convert solar radiation energy into different forms of energy.
- Create interference radiation.
- Create polarized light.

- Provide a low solar radiation environment for humans.
- Influence human behaviors.
- Influence human development.
- Regulate the ground level solar radiation environment.
- Create an environment for other organisms, such as fungi, to grow.
- Appear to create resonant electromagnetic energy.
- Appear to have the ability to communicate.
- Fertilize the ground around them by dropping their leaves in fall.
- Cool the local environment.
- Provide shade.
- Provide regulation of gasses to the atmosphere.
- Trap water.
- Provide water absorption during rains.
- Help prevent flooding during rains.
- Release water into the soil.
- Provide water vapor regulation to the atmosphere.
- Create a DC voltage on the tree canopy.
- Act as transceiver antenna systems.

Trees are being reported to be under stress around the world. It is important that we identify and rectify these stresses at the earliest opportunity.

"If you think in terms of a year, plant a seed; if in terms of ten years, plant trees; if in terms of 100 years, teach the people."

Confucius

Light Forensics © Steven Magee

Plant Light

Plants are affected by many factors. Climate change is changing rainfall, humidity, air composition, solar radiation, heating and cooling. Plants are sensitive to any of these factors. When all of the factors start to change at once, it may lead to devastation in the plant world.

Seeds only germinate in a narrow range of temperatures. If the temperature changes and is outside of this range then germination will not occur.

Seeds will only germinate when there is sufficient light passing through the tree canopy. It appears that nature automatically fills holes in the tree canopy.

Seeds need a certain level of water to germinate. If this water level changes then they may not germinate.

Plant leaves change with different solar radiation levels. The same plant will change the color, shape, and size of the leaves to match the level of solar radiation that it receives. There is a limit to how adaptable each plant is and if the radiation gets outside of its range, the plant will start to show stress and may die.

Plants that appear to be well suited to constantly high levels of solar radiation appear to be those of the cactus family. They also have the ability to tolerate extremely low rainfall levels. Some of the plants in these desert environments appear to have the ability to move their leaves to match the level of solar radiation. When it is very high, they close them together and when it is low, they open their leaves to the Sun.

A changed radiation environment for plants may have the following effects:

- Leaf changes.
- Growth changes.

- Accelerated or retarded growth.
- Stress.
- Reproduction issues.
- Depression.
- Death.

Loss of many varieties of plants may cascade down the food chain to the humans. As the plants die off, the life support system for humans will start to reduce and human starvation may result.

Plant life is like the canary in the cage. When it starts to die off, we know we have problems. To ignore plant die off would be like the human race committing suicide. Human extinction would surely follow.

Plant types typically fall into the following classifications:

- Full Sun.
- Partial Sun.
- Shade.
- Indoors.

They can also be classed into these types:

- Tropical.
- Dry.
- Mild temperate.
- Continental.

Humans can also be put into these classifications:

Light Forensics © Steven Magee

- Tropical – Black skin.
- Dry – Dark skin.
- Mild temperate – Light skin.
- Continental – White.

The human plant classification appears to be a shade plant. We see this by looking at our closest relative, the monkey. All monkeys are found dwelling in forests. The reason why the skin changes color over many generations is to genetically adapt to the radiation environment. Dark skinned people need to be outdoors in a high radiation environment in the tropics to be in good health while light skinned people need to be outdoors nearer to the poles.

The color of light is known to cause plant problems. Red light can cause germination while far red can prevent it. The last light exposure that the plant receives can have profound effects on its development. The sensitivity of plants to light can feed into many aspects of their development.

Most plant shoots will grow towards a source of blue light, but not towards a source of red light. This is called "phototropism". Green leaves have chlorophyll in them that absorb both the red and blue wavelengths of light. The leaves look green because they reject the green content of light. Trees absorb the red light but reject the far red, so the plants underneath trees tend to be adapted to use the far red light.

Many plants are adapted to the length of the day. This is called "Photoperiodism". Some like to flower on long days, while others like to flower on short days. There are plants that like to flower on average length days and others that flower simply when they have reached a certain size. The classifications are:

- Long day.

Light Forensics © Steven Magee

- Short day.
- Intermediate day.
- Neutral day.

It is interesting to note that exposure to a pulse of light during the night can upset the rhythm of the plant and either prevent it from flowering or cause it to flower, depending on the species.

Artificially extending the day may cause extended growth cycles on the plant. The strength of the response to the plant depends on the type of light source used. The strongest response to the least response is:

1. Incandescent.
2. High pressure sodium vapor.
3. Metal halide.
4. Cool white florescent.
5. Clear mercury vapor.

There are no doubts that artificial lights affect plants. Human genetics have adapted to the plant life and radiation levels that has surrounded them for thousands of years. Any human that significantly changes their environment is likely to become ill outside of their genetically adapted environment. Changing the plant life and lighting exposures is likely to have profound effects on the human.

If you have significantly changed your environment by moving away from it and are ill, assuming that you cannot recover your health with natural lifestyle changes, then you should consider returning back to your genetic environment. This will put you back into genetic harmony.

"Lethargics are to be laid in the light, and exposed to the rays of the Sun for the disease is gloom."

Aretaeus

Fertility Light

Over-population has put an enormous strain on the Earth. The massive crop farming that must take place to support the large number of humans has significantly changed the rural landscape. It has led to the massive destruction of trees globally, a corresponding release of trapped gasses into the environment and an addition to the atmosphere of trapped fossil fuel exhaust gasses.

Human population has now reached a point globally that it should now start to be controlled and possibly reduced over the coming generations.

Stimulation of animals and plants by certain light exposures is known to increase fertility and breeding cycles. It is likely that the modern human today is far more fertile than those of the past. It does not surprise me that the explosion in human population of the Earth has coincided with the introduction of artificial light and the removal of the trees around the world. The human is now exposed to very unnatural forms of light that it did not develop in harmony with. I call this effect:

Electromagnetic Population Growth

The exploding growth rate of the population is shown in the next diagram.

"We already have the statistics for the future: the growth percentages of pollution, overpopulation, desertification. The future is already in place."
Gunther Grass

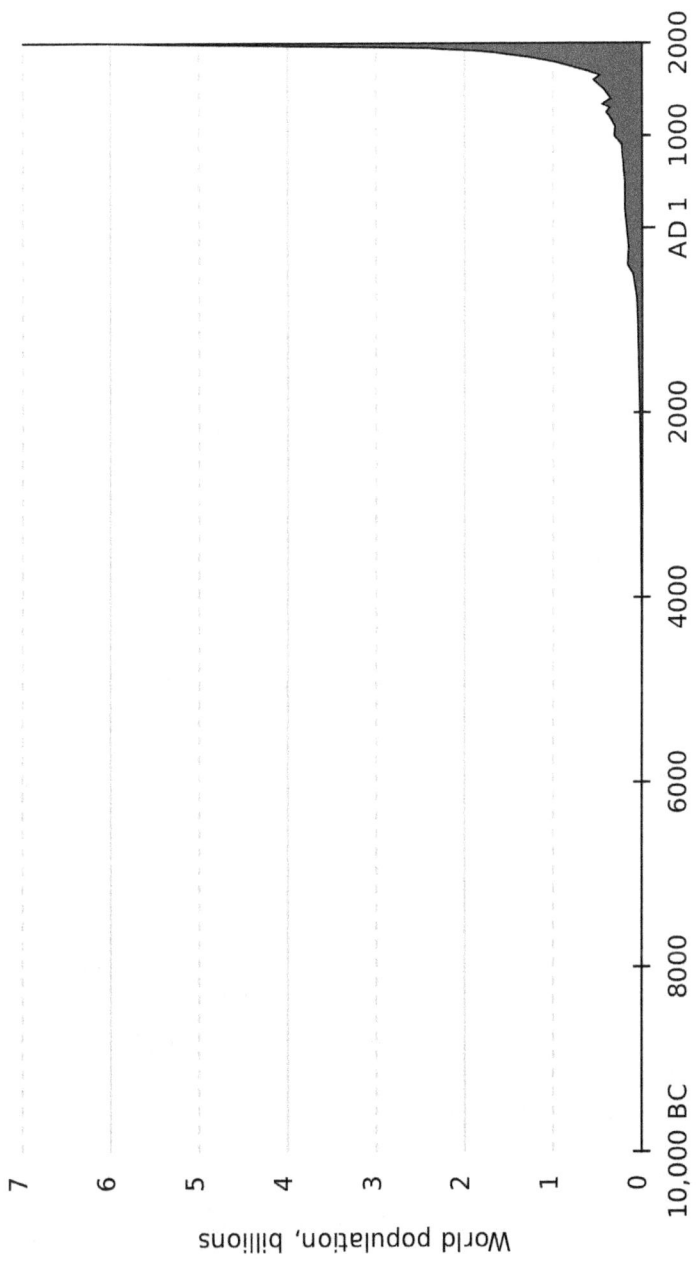

Light Forensics © Steven Magee

Farm Light

The trees were removed to make way for the open fields that we now have to grow the crops needed to support the humans in the cities. The open crop fields are generally not natural, they are engineered by humans.

Open fields that are not planted and are just dirt will absorb solar radiation energy. This will heat the soil which in turn will transfer that heat to the air above it.

Open fields of soil or crops generally have a much higher reflectivity than trees. This effect can be seen from airplanes and satellite images. This means that less solar energy is absorbed by the field compared to a forest. A net solar energy loss occurs due to the field reflecting solar energy back into the atmosphere and some of that solar energy ends up returning into Space.

The reflected solar energy that does not make it back into Space ends up being absorbed by the atmosphere. This is an extra addition of energy to the atmosphere that should appear as an air temperature increase. It sounds a lot like global warming.

We should probably be growing crops in the shade of native trees. Some types of crops that are not grown in the shade of trees may end up with a level of solar poisoning in them from excessive solar radiation exposure. It would be undesirable for humans to eat such food.

The solar poisoning effect may also exist in meat and fish that are farmed using modern agricultural techniques. It may be important to grow these foods in natural environments that provide natural shade cover.

"Globalized industrialized food is not cheap: it is too costly for the Earth, for the farmers, for our health. The Earth can no longer carry the burden of groundwater mining, pesticide

pollution, disappearance of species and destabilization of the climate. Farmers can no longer carry the burden of debt, which is inevitable in industrial farming with its high costs of production. It is incapable of producing safe, culturally appropriate, tasty, quality food. And it is incapable of producing enough food for all because it is wasteful of land, water and energy. Industrial agriculture uses ten times more energy than it produces. It is thus ten times less efficient."

Vandana Shiva

Light Forensics © Steven Magee

Fossil Fuel Light

Fossil fuels are widely used throughout the world. The easy fuels have been accessed and depleted. Now we are developing the more difficult sources of these fuels with the associated increased risks that this creates.

So what exactly are fossil fuels? The correct answer is that no one really knows. They may not even be made from fossils. The correct name for these fuels is "substances from unknown origin". They are toxic to humans. Abiogenic and abiotic are terms that can be used to describe these fuels. Their meaning is "Without Life".

The fossil fuel industry has created the biggest threat to human extinction and the extinction of the majority of the Earth's animal and plant species and they have done this in a period of just over a century.

When we drill into the Earth and bring the trapped coal, gas and oil to the surface, it is burned and releases the exhaust gasses from it into the atmosphere. Those exhaust gasses may be radioactive. These add to the composition of the atmosphere. The important concept here is "Add". No one really understands how adding large amounts of exhaust gasses into a stable atmosphere affects it. It is a mystery.

The atmosphere is a really thin layer on the surface of the Earth. To add large amounts of previously trapped exhaust gasses to it is like gambling with our future. If the gamble does not work out well, the effects could be serious and may not be able to be undone.

The extraction and burning of fossil fuels is strongly linked to global warming. Humans are adding large amounts of exhaust gasses to an atmosphere that took millions of years to develop in harmony with humans. It may reach a critical point in the future where the human body can not keep pace with the changing composition of the atmosphere. This will place the human body under continual stress and may push it into a diseased state and onto premature death.

Many prominent scientists and engineers have been warning about the problem of burning fossil fuels for many decades. Even the inventor of AC electricity was warning about it. Nikola Tesla states *"It is our duty to coming generations to leave this store of energy intact for them, or at least not to touch it until we shall have perfected processes for burning coal more efficiently"*. It is clear that Nikola Tesla was an advocate of renewable natural energy sources, such as solar, wind and water.

We have already witnessed the effects of a poisonous local atmosphere with the human habit of smoking. A poisonous global atmosphere may eventually lead to widespread human disease and onto a possible human extinction. If this happens, nature will take over and reforest the planet, restoring the balance once again and another less invasive species will become dominant.

There is a significant problem associated with burning large quantities of fossil fuels into the atmosphere. This pollution will change the solar radiation transmission of the atmosphere and lead to an unnatural radiation environment at the ground level where we all live. Once the radiation environment has been significantly changed by these emissions, then we will be in a new era of evolution. It appears that we have already entered that era some time ago.

The problem with adding lots of extra molecules to a stable atmosphere is that it may create filtering, polarization, diffraction and interference of the solar radiation transmission from Space to the surface of the Earth. If this happens, then it may increase the illness and disease rates in humans. In some parts of the world solar radiation filtering, polarization, diffraction and interference may already be occurring.

We are now seeing the more difficult fuels being developed, such as tar sands and fracking natural gas, and the fossil fuel industry is entering a new era in its toxic history. Such toxic fuel sources would not have been developed a few decades ago and this highlights how desperate the energy industry is to source its fuel supplies.

There is massive pollution entering the atmosphere on a daily basis and it is becoming more toxic, to the point that it appears to be harming mankind. Fossil fuel use should be stopped as we know it is toxic to humanity.

"Practically every environmental problem we have can be traced to our addiction to fossil fuels, primarily oil."

Dennis Weaver

Polluted Light

Light pollution comes in many forms and some of these are:

- Unnaturally high levels of solar radiation.
- Unnaturally low levels of solar radiation.
- Unnaturally filtered solar radiation.
- Polarized solar radiation.
- Diffracted solar radiation.
- Interference solar radiation.
- Man-made light sources.
- Extraction and burning of fossil fuels.
- Industrial processes.
- Chemicals.
- Smoke.
- Heat.
- Water vapor.
- Dust.
- Volcanoes.

Why is pollution a problem for solar radiation? Well, it is not just the levels of carbon dioxide that went up, it is the levels of almost everything else that went up too! There is far more water vapor stored in the atmosphere from the over use of modern crop farming techniques that use irrigation, and this is just one of the many examples of things that have changed the atmospheric gasses. The problem with far more more molecules in the atmosphere is that they will do a number of things:

Light Forensics © Steven Magee

- Block the Sun's rays.
- Heat up.
- Start moving more energetically.
- Create solar radiation transmission effects.
- Transmission effects may lead to illness, disease, and cancer in humans, and throughout the natural world.

But it doesn't stop there. The addition of certain chemicals to the atmosphere will destroy wavelengths of light and it may only be a matter of time before one of these wavelengths of light that is critical for human survival is eliminated. This is called:

The Extinction Wavelength

The extinction wavelength of light may be achieved in the near future that may lead to the mass extinction of the human race. So, for sunlight and human health, atmospheric pollution is an extremely serious problem! It is entirely possible that we may achieve the extinction wavelength within the next fifty years and that will mark the point of the start of the end for humanity.

With each passing year the solar radiation spectrum is slowly changing. As the atmosphere fills up with molecules from pollution we will start to move towards increasing solar radiation transmission effects from the Sun. Increased sunlight filtering and interference is likely to increase the disease rates in all living organisms, including the human.

Unnatural levels of solar radiation should be expected to induce illness and disease into almost everything. The human, bird, animal, plant and marine kingdoms will all be greatly affected. Unfortunately, the unnatural levels of solar radiation in modern society appear to be man-made.

Light Forensics © Steven Magee

The following picture was taken from an airplane window at cruising altitude and shows a white Sun and an atmospheric filtered orange sunlight reflection from the ocean!

Light Forensics © Steven Magee

The Sun as Viewed from an Airplane.

This picture was taken from an airplane window at cruising altitude in the Pacific ocean near Hawaii. Note the white Sun and orange reflection below.

Light Forensics © Steven Magee

So how can it be prevented? Simply by stopping all man-made emissions into the atmosphere, rivers and oceans. Rapid reforestation of the planet with trees would essentially restore the lungs of the Earth and start to trap the man-made emissions that are present in the atmosphere.

Just like humans, the planet has two lungs. The other is the ocean. The pollution into the ocean needs to stop so that the ocean can recover and restore its lung capacity.

Sunlight is regarded as having the color of white. It is quite possible that thousands of years ago the sunrises and sunsets were white, not the reds and oranges that we have today. White is regarded a pure. Unfiltered sunlight matches this color.

It is recommended that we move as quickly as we can back to an atmosphere that does not excessively filter the sunlight and change its color. This appears to be required for humanity to return to a healthy society.

By stopping pollution today, we can start creating the world that our children can thrive in. If we don't make these changes quickly, then there may be no future for our children. Humanity will most likely go extinct.

So how can we gauge the progression of air pollution? The answer turns out to be relatively easy. Humans have been painting sunsets and moon-sets for hundreds of years in their artwork. Fortunately, much of this artwork has been kept in pristine condition and is available to view.

When reviewing the artwork of sunsets and moon-sets, we see that the orange or red sunset appears to be a relatively modern phenomenon. Prior to this, sunsets and moon-sets did not appear to be orange or red. They were relatively white.

Evidence of atmospheric pollution will be at its worst when the Sun or the Moon is near to the horizon. This is due to the radiation from these objects passing through the thickest part of the atmosphere. This is called high air mass in the scientific community. The radiation is subjected to the most atmospheric filtration at this time. Air mass is 1 when the Sun is at zenith and down at the horizon it is near to 38. This means that the solar radiation receives approximately 38 times more atmospheric filtration at sunset.

Pollution causes the visible light to turn orange or red due to the filtering effects of pollution on this light. The more pollution there is, the redder it will look. This can be seen on the island of Hawaii where the Kilauea volcano is erupting and pumping out gasses into the environment. The sunsets on this island are red, like the color of blood.

This is a problem near the poles, due to the Sun being lower in the sky. The sunlight is subjected to much more filtration by the atmosphere for much longer periods of time. This may be unhealthy for people who live nearer to the poles.

Filtering solar radiation with pollution is a bad idea.

A good example of pollution in the atmosphere is on the cover of my first book "Solar Photovoltaic Design for Residential, Commercial and Utility Systems". This picture was taken from the summit of Kitt Peak National Observatory in Sells, Arizona, USA. At an elevation of approximately 6,875 feet, we can see a deep orange sunset. This is shown on the next page.

This sunset several hundred years ago probably would have been a white sunset. Orange and red sunsets are characteristic of a polluted atmosphere. Viewing the midday Sun through smoke also produces an orange or red view of it.

It is interesting that smoking causes cancer. Could it be that smokers are having cancer induced into them by the same effects as pollution creates with solar radiation?

"Our meaning is to make our little planet Earth a better place to live, to stop wars, disarm nuclear missiles, to stop diseases, AIDS, plague, cancer and to stop pollution."

Uri Geller

Light Forensics © Steven Magee

The Orange Sunset from Kitt Peak.

Light Forensics © Steven Magee

Atmospheric Pollution

Atmospheric pollution can cause Sun filtering, polarization, diffraction and interference effects.

Satellite Light

Several decades ago the Earth only had one moon orbiting it. Today it has several thousand! The development of the Space industry has led to massive amounts of satellites to be put in orbit. However, the Space industry did not do its homework prior to developing this field.

Mankind has known for thousands of years that when the Moon eclipses the Sun, many strange behaviors are observed in animals and plants. All of the cycles go off and some plants will open their flowers and others will close them. The animal behaviors show a state of confusion. Animals will wake up and others will go to sleep. Birds and bees stop flying. It does not matter what time of day the eclipse occurs, animal behavior is affected, so it is not just a change in lighting levels or heat that does this.

What an eclipse of the Sun does is to create a very strange radiation environment on Earth. The animals and plants are reacting to the changed electromagnetic radiation environment. Light and heat is just a small part of that changed environment.

The same effect appears to happen with satellites. The International Space Station is so large now, that it is the biggest thing in Space that can be photographed passing across the surface of the Sun, other than the moon. It is far larger than the sunspots! Every time a satellite passes in front of the Sun, the electromagnetic environment is changed on the ground below. The effects of this are currently unknown.

However, in recent years a problem in the bees has shown up called "Bee Colony Collapse Disorder" and it may well have a link to man-made satellite eclipses of the Sun that cause diffraction and interference radiation to occur.

The other problem with satellites is that they are continually bombarding the Earth with electromagnetic radiation! No one is quite sure what types of radiation that they are broadcasting as there are so many of them, many of which are secret military satellites. However, it is a fact that it is diverse.

This diverse radiation is an addition of electromagnetic radiation on the surface of the Earth. Today, there is nowhere on the surface of the Earth that is free from it. The Earth has complete satellite coverage. This is shown on the next page.

Light Forensics © Steven Magee

Satellite Electromagnetic Radiation

The Earth has complete satellite coverage.

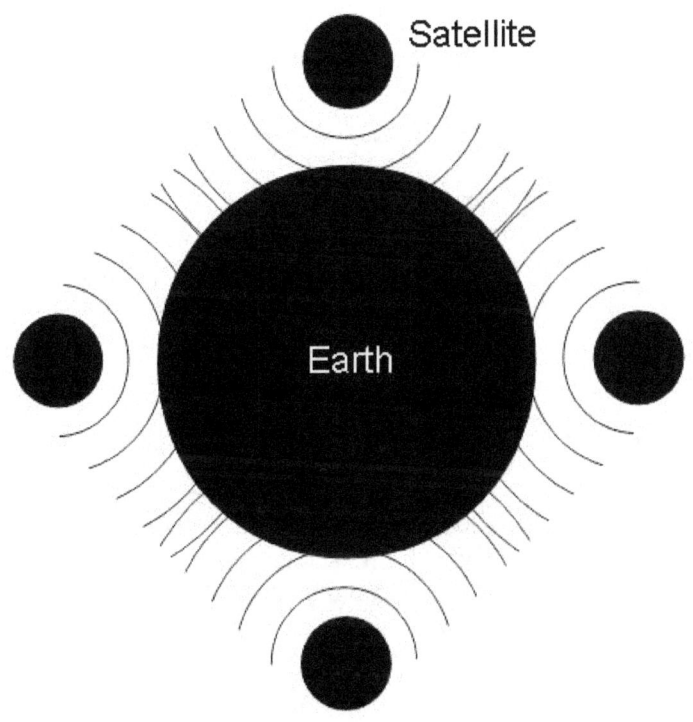

This is somewhat concerning, given the extensive denial about the health effects of man-made electromagnetic radiation. There is only one European country that appears to acknowledge it and that is Sweden. In Sweden, approximately 300,000 people are registered as having electromagnetic hypersensitivity. It clearly is a problem that is not unique to Sweden!

Unfortunately for the modern human, the development of the satellite industry took place without understanding these problems and today, it may actually be one of the biggest problems facing the future of humanity!

A scary thought about satellites is that once a nation has complete global coverage of the Earth, if they were to broadcast the correct types of electromagnetic radiation frequencies to the surface of the Earth, they could feasibly cause massive species extinction. This is called:

Satellite Extinction

The military has already identified frequencies of energy that are harmful to human health and developed them for use in war zones. It is probably a feature that is already present on secret military satellites.

I expect to see many countries in the future to be requesting the removal of satellites from their field of view of the sky. Satellites are the latest pollutant to be identified as a potential human health hazard.

"The U.S. spends over $2 trillion dollars on health care each year, of which about 78% is from people with chronic illnesses, without adequately exploring and understanding what factors —including EMF/RF—contribute to imbalances in peoples' bodies' in the first place. After reading The BioInitiative Report, it should come as no surprise to policymakers, given the continually increasing levels of EMF/RF exposures in our environment, that close to 50% of Americans now live with a

chronic illness. I grieve for people who needlessly suffer these illnesses and hold out the hope that our government leaders will become more cognizant of the role electromagnetic factors are playing in disease, health care costs and the erosion of quality of life and productivity in America."

Camilla Rees, MBA

Light Forensics © Steven Magee

Man-Made Reflections

Man-made solar reflections have raised the solar radiation levels in society. These occur from many sources and we will list some of them here:

- Light colored paints.
- Glossy paints.
- Smooth engineered surfaces.
- Glass.
- Mirrors.
- Reflective glass.
- Roofing materials.
- Cars and transportation systems.
- Tall structures.

There are many sources of man-made reflections and you should become accustomed to assessing your optical environment. Learn to identify these reflective items and assess their impact on solar radiation.

Reflected light is also known to interfere with wildlife and water based birds are known to land of reflective surfaces such as roads, fields, and greenhouses. They all look like water from up above.

We will now look into what you will find in a modern man-made environment.

"Concentrate all your thoughts upon the work at hand. The Sun's rays do not burn until brought to a focus."
Alexander Graham Bell

Structure Radiation

Tall structures can be a problem as they may reflect a lot of solar radiation to the ground around them. This effect increases as you get closer to them. Structures appear to have the ability to modify the solar radiation by creating:

- Unnaturally high radiation power levels.
- Changed solar radiation spectrum.
- Light filtering.
- Light polarization.
- Light diffraction.
- Light interference.

Structures such as:

- Antennas.
- Dams.
- Wind turbines.
- Solar power systems.
- Power stations.
- Power transmission and distribution lines.
- Power poles.
- Domes.
- Tall buildings.
- Lampposts.
- Bridges.

- Street signs.
- Storage tanks.
- Cranes.
- Chemical plants.
- Industrial buildings.
- Pyramids.
- Roofs visible from the ground.

Many types of structures create these solar radiation effects and the above list is just a short sample of the structures that can do this.

Dr. John Nash Ott found that increasing the ultraviolet energy content of light can cause cells to rupture. You need to be careful in areas of unnaturally high ultraviolet radiation due to the effect that it may have on the human body. The peak areas in society for these ultraviolet effects appears to occur around glass covered buildings. When around such buildings, you should wear a hat, cover up, and pass through the areas of high ultraviolet radiation quickly.

My plant growth experiments are indicating that accelerated growth patterns can occur in unnaturally high solar radiation environments. It is likely that this accelerated growth pattern would occur in animals and plants that were subjected to it. Solar radiation accelerated growth patterns in humans requires further study. It has been noticed that USA children are entering puberty a couple of years earlier than a few decades ago and it may be related to this effect.

In areas around tall glass covered buildings, the sky is very different. If you look up at certain times of the day, you may actually see two or more Sun's in the sky! You will see the real Sun and one or more reflected Sun's. This increases the ground based radiation levels and the effect on human health is not fully understood yet. Until it is, it pays to exercise caution around it. It is called the "Multiple-Sun Effect".

One can only wonder what extended exposure to unnaturally high levels of solar radiation to the human mind and body would eventually cause?

This effect was headline news in 2010 and the press called it the "Las Vegas Death Ray" due to a curved, mirrored, glass covered hotel in Las Vegas exhibiting the problem. The radiation levels on the ground were getting so high that the plastic drinking cups and plastic shopping bags were melting! It is interesting to note that the USA press published this story after receiving copies of my book "Solar Reflections for Architects, Engineers and Human Health" some months earlier. The basics of the article and diagrams that were featured appeared to match those in my book. Indeed, my book even has a chapter on Las Vegas! No references to my research nor royalties were ever given to me by the USA press. This intellectual property was registered with the USA Copyright Office under registration number TXu 1-699-149 on June 14, 2010. The story appeared to be first published on September 27, 2010 by the USA media and many media sources picked up on the story and reported it over the following days.

Having looked through my books, I first copyrighted the mirrored building "Multiple-Sun" lensing effect on April 25th, 2010. It was reported in my book "Solar Irradiance and Insolation for Power Systems" which is covered by the USA copyright TXu 1-688-857. You can see the mirrored building lensing effect on some of my book covers, as it makes for an interesting picture!

Is this a case of intellectual property theft by corporate controlled media? It is interesting to note that the corporate news media that received copies of my book never acknowledged it.

The effect of focusing the Sun to set ships on fire was documented by Archimedes a long time ago as the "Archimedes Death Ray". He did not discuss using buildings to create the effect and simply documented using large mirrors to focus solar radiation onto invading ships at sea to set them on fire. The television program "Myth Busters" have tried to recreate the Archimedes death ray a number of times and have repeatedly failed to demonstrate that the mirrors that Archimedes describes could set wooden ships on fire.

The following pages show some of the Solar effects that you should be aware of:

Light Forensics © Steven Magee

The "Multiple-Sun" Effect

Building glass can create the "Multiple-Sun" effect.

Building Solar Lensing

The multiple-Sun reflection of many Suns from a tall, mirrored, curved glass office building.

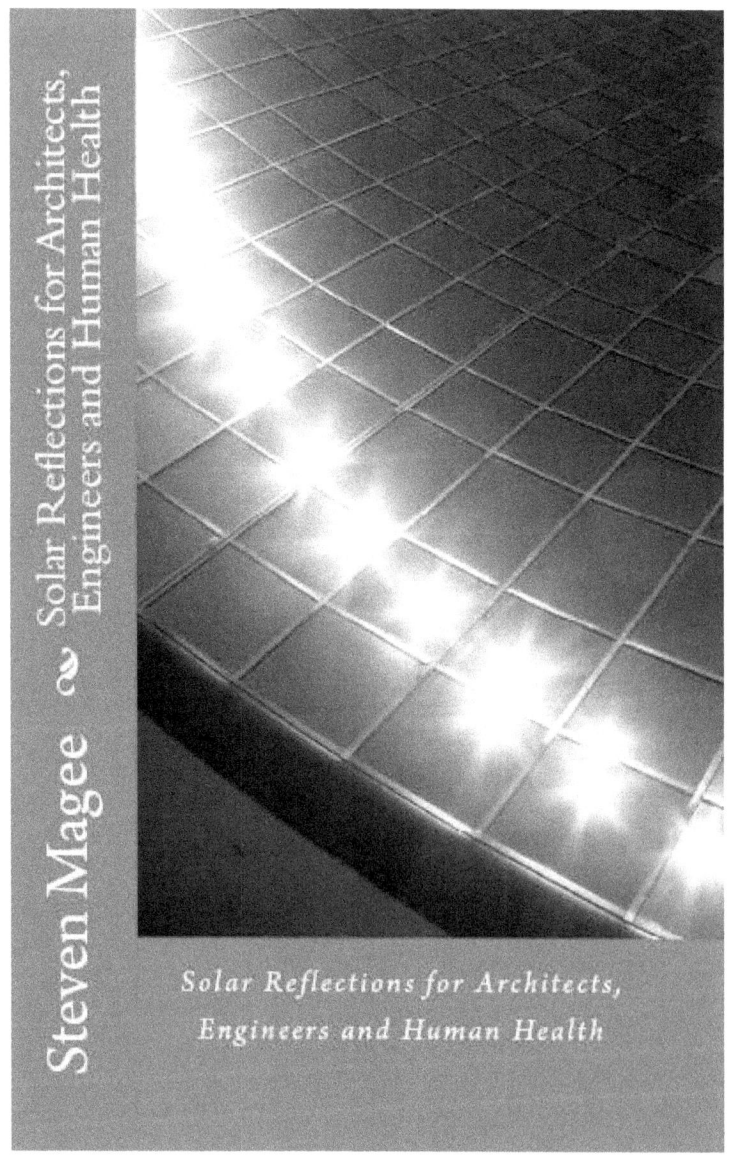

Light Forensics © Steven Magee

The "Multiple-Shadow" Effect

The "Multiple-Shadow" effect accompanies the "Multiple-Sun" effect. The bright area on the right is higher in solar radiation power than Space!

You should try to avoid being near tall structures during the main solar radiation hours of the day. Particularly near solar noon these effects are at their maximum. If you work in one of these structures, you should try and stay inside during your work day to avoid passing through the high levels of solar radiation that they may create around them.

It is plausible that the structures in your environment may be able to affect your health. As such, you should be careful around anything man-made that is taller than a single story home until more is known on the subject.

It is recommended that the construction of tall structures be avoided and that if a large structure is required that it be located below ground level, such as in an old surface mine.

If a large structure is built above ground, then it should probably be covered in plant growth.

The optical diagram of how buildings act as lenses is shown on the next page.

Building Reflections

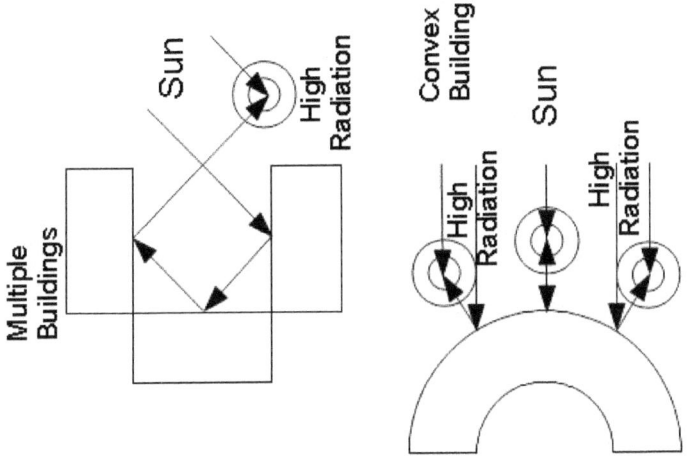

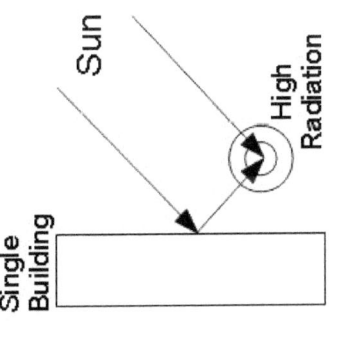

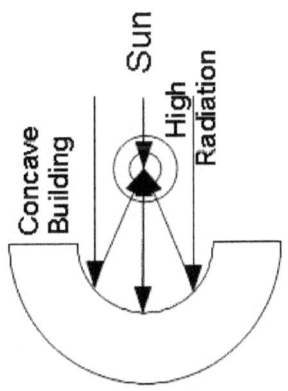

Power transmission and distribution lines should be routed underground wherever possible. This will prevent solar radiation effects from occurring.

It is an interesting observation that almost all pyramids in the world have been found abandoned. The pyramid structure generates high levels of horizontal solar radiation around it. The human brain, eyes, organs, and body appear not to be designed to deal with these increased horizontal reflections.

This is shown on the next page.

Pyramids Focusing Radiation

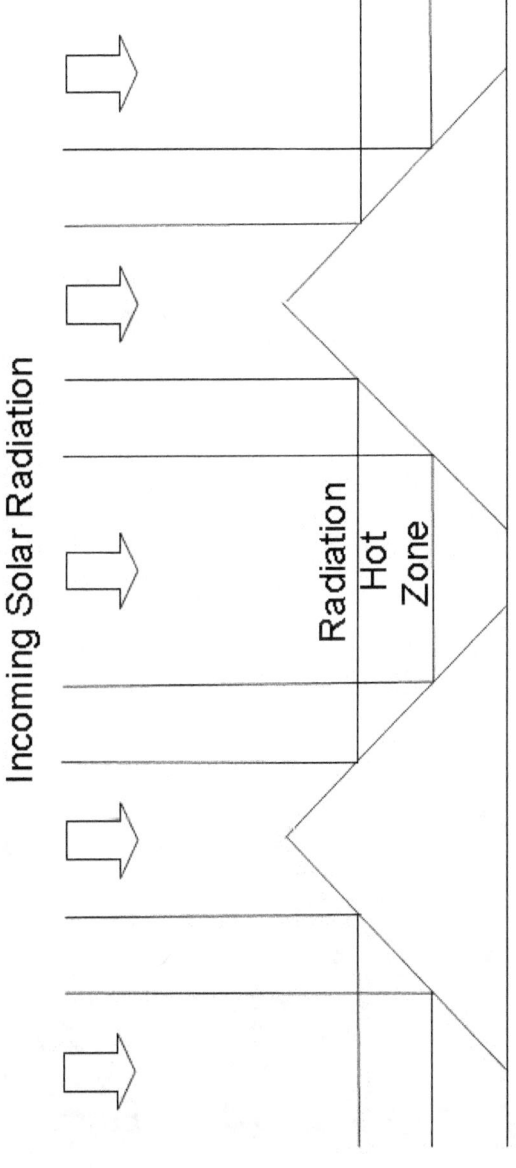

Light Forensics © Steven Magee

Pyramid Horizontal Solar Radiation

The pyramid is shown reflecting the Sun near solar noon.

Light Forensics © Steven Magee

Tall buildings may be an issue to human health on a number of fronts. When you are on the upper floors and have a clear view of the world, everything around you also has a clear view of you too! This includes:

- Solar radiation.
- Radiation reflections.
- Wireless radiation.

All types of radiation are more powerful with a direct line of sight to their source.

If you live in one of these buildings, it is recommended that you block the view with live plant life. They will absorb and modify the radiation levels for you. You should think of plant life as your guardian angel. They should make you feel good and, if you have flowers, they will look really pretty.

The following pages show some of the typical objects that can affect radiation transmission.

"Do you see how the god always hurls his bolts at the greatest houses and the tallest trees. For he is wont to thwart whatever is greater than the rest."

Herodotus

Light Forensics © Steven Magee

Power Pole Interference

The solar radiation distorts around the lines and poles and causes reflections, polarization, diffraction and interference effects.

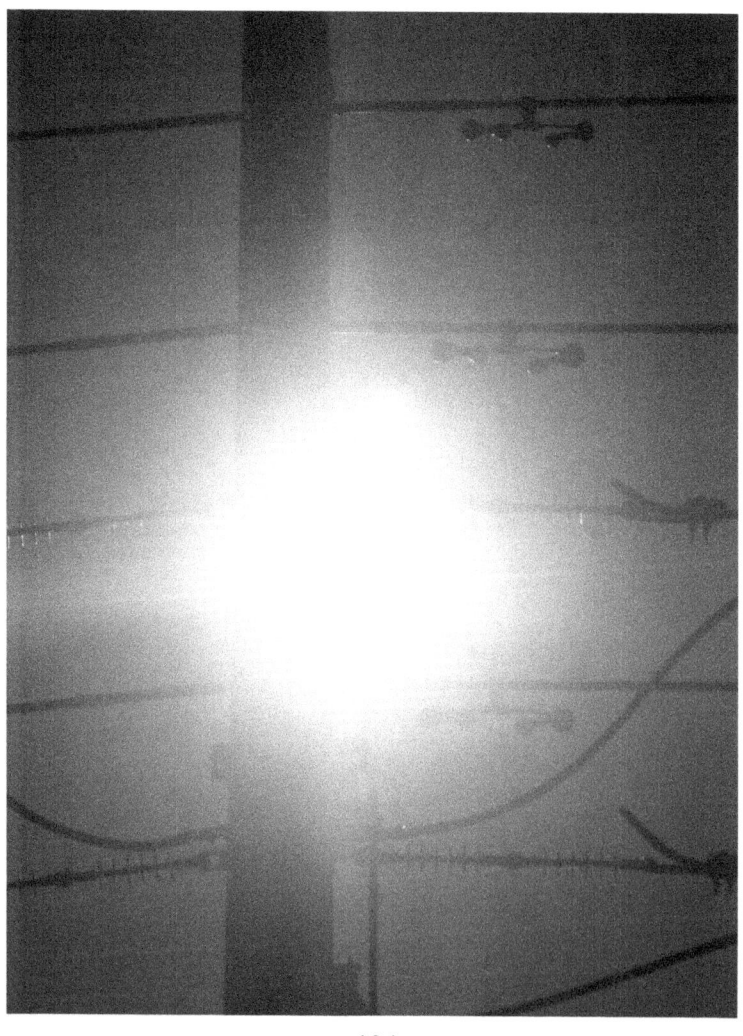

Light Forensics © Steven Magee

Lamppost Interference

The solar radiation bleeds into the lamppost and causes reflections, polarization, diffraction and interference effects.

Light Forensics © Steven Magee

Cell Phone Tower Interference

Towers and antennas may create reflections, polarization, diffraction and interference effects.

Light Forensics © Steven Magee

Alternate Energy

While alternate energy sources seem appealing, they have their problems too.

Solar Energy

Solar photovoltaics has issues that are currently emerging:

- Engineers and designers who do not understand the optical environment that they are designing systems for nor solar photovoltics.
- Construction permits being issued by officials who do not understand solar photovoltaics nor optics.
- Poorly designed systems may overload and go on fire.
- DC arcing and DC fires as equipment ages and breaks down.
- Inverter electromagnetic field emissions.
- System electromagnetic field emissions into the human environment.
- Unnatural solar radiation levels in the human environment from solar reflections. A solar power worker may develop radiation sickness from working outdoors around these systems.
- Solar glare.
- Increased thermal activity above the system.
- Micro-climates may be created in areas that the systems are installed into.

Light Forensics © Steven Magee

- Harmonics.
- Dirty electricity.
- Stray voltage, stray current and stray frequency.
- Intermittent power production.
- Daytime only power production.
- Seasonal power production.
- Installation into environments that are unsuited to the technology.
- The industry staying relatively silent about the problems.

Solar energy systems generally operate with low efficiencies and the solar radiation that is not converted into energy ends up either being reflected, diffracted, interfered with, or turned into heat. They are all are undesirable. Heat may contribute to the effects of climate change. The reflections, polarization, diffraction, and interference effects may raise the solar radiation levels around the systems to unnatural levels. Commercial and utility solar energy systems are essentially very large atmospheric plate heaters that cover extremely large areas of land. They may contribute to climate change rather than reduce it. The processes involved in making them may be toxic to the environment.

The book "Challenging the Chip: Labor Rights and Environmental Justice in the Global Electronics Industry" covers some of these production problems.

I can tell you that during working full time at a very large utility solar photovoltaic power plant for a couple of months, my health went terrible. My body was filled with aches and pains, and my sleep cycle was off. My concentration was off and my ability to handle stressful situations was compromised. My senses would not be working right and I found that I would make simple mistakes for no rational reason. I occasionally would find myself in a state of confusion when trying to do simple tasks. The solar power plant was producing high levels of electronically generated harmonic energy and this was definitely a factor in the health issues that I was seeing.

After I left the electronic utility power plant, I noticed that my memory was having issues as well. I could not remember telephone numbers, alarm codes, computer passwords, and my ability to do basic mathematics was compromised. It was one of the most distressing experiences that I have ever had! It slowly improved after performing the radiation detoxification process. It took about a year for things to significantly improve from the toxic exposures of the system. It is interesting that Nikola Tesla also reported this memory loss effect and also recovered many of his memories over time.

This appears to be a form of Dementia and this leads me to conclude that dementia may actually be curable.

I had noticed aggression, fatigue, and memory problems in the staff at the site. In conversations with them, they were also reporting insomnia, general aches and pains.

The solar reflection problem is shown in the next picture and this raises the solar radiation levels in the human environment to unnaturally high levels.

Light Forensics © Steven Magee

The reflections from solar modules raise the radiation levels significantly in the human environment.

Some of these problems also apply to wind energy systems. In particular, electronic power generation by inverters is a feature shared by both. Electronic power generation into the grid is relatively new and the long term human health consequences of electronically generated harmonic energy are not yet fully understood.

Wind Power

In the wind power industry, the following documentation has arrived in recent years:

- The Wind Farm Scam by John Etherington.
- Wind Turbine Syndrome: A Report on a Natural Experiment by Nina Pierpont.
- Windfall (2010): A film by Laura Israel.

Between them, they do a good job of explaining the factual problems in both energy production and the detrimental human health and nature issues around the wind turbines.

These systems are very large and tall. Tall structures may cause solar radiation reflections, polarization, diffraction and interference effects which are undesirable, as they may raise the radiation levels around them. They also kill flying animals, such as birds, insects and bats, as their blade tips can travel at approximately 250 miles per hour. If you examine a wind turbine blade, it may be covered in splattered bugs, just like the front of your car. The areas around wind turbines are becoming nature dead zones, due to:

- Air pressure waves that they create. People who live up to ten miles downwind of these turbines may complain about the noise that they can make.

- Infra-sound.
- Wind turbines extract their energy from wind and affect the natural wind systems.
- Optically, they cause flicker to occur which the human body may be sensitive to. This may cause health problems in people who have a view of them.
- Vibrations in the ground around them.
- They may create atmospheric energy interference.

Tidal

Tidal systems disrupt the natural flow of water and may affect the underwater environment of the sea life.

Dams

These disrupt the natural flow of water and upset the life within the river. They create massive water evaporation into the atmosphere.

Wave

These systems have not been perfected yet and disrupt the natural flow of ocean water and ocean life.

Nuclear

Natural energy that has not been perfected. The mining and processing of the fuel is highly destructive to the environment. It generates a lot of waste heat, water evaporation and highly toxic waste that no one knows what to do with. The highly toxic waste will be around for thousands of years. The highly toxic waste is a disaster waiting to happen, as we have seen with the Fukushima nuclear disaster in Japan. Unfortunately, it appears that we may be leaving a highly poisonous discovery for a future generation that may not be aware of the dangers contained within the storage containers.

While alternate energy systems appear appealing, they quite often are installed for public relations and investor purposes, rather than to generate significant quantities of energy into the utility grid.

The current generation of solar and wind power systems generally introduce instability into the electrical utility grid system with their intermittent power generation characteristics and electronically generated harmonic energy. Generally, there has to be a peaking gas turbine plant near to the very large utility installations to offset these unstable energy generation systems. Unfortunately, these peaking power plants are the lowest efficiency way of generating fossil fuel energy into the utility grid. A wind or solar farm combined with a peaking power plant may not actually save any fossil fuel emissions when compared to a high efficiency conventional power plant. In some cases, they may actually use more energy!

I'm not sure why we ever moved away from natural surface fuels. They are completely renewable. It is suggested that our dependance on energy be returned to natural bio-fuels, such as wood, at the earliest possible opportunity.

Humans are displaying an addiction to energy that appears to be like drug addiction. It rules their lives. Humans should be weaned off energy consumption in order to reduce this unnatural dependance that has been formed. If it continues then it may destroy the atmosphere and, by association, lead to the extinction of humanity.

Homes should have trees placed around them to help keep them cool and reduce the air conditioning loads on the electrical grid. Ideally, homes should be located under the tree canopy due to the stable environmental conditions that it creates for humans.

The book "Sparking a Worldwide Energy Revolution" gives a good overview to the energy problems of today and possible ways forward.

The book "The False Promise of Green Energy" gives an overview of the green energy industry.

"The facts are there that we have created, man has, a self-inflicted wound through global warming."

Arnold Schwarzenegger

Light Forensics © Steven Magee

Glass

The use of glass for windows in homes is relatively modern. In past years glass was rougher and this can be seen in older buildings. The older glass appears to distort the images that pass through it and defects can be seen.

Float glass was later developed in the 1960's and is a very smooth engineered surface. Most modern glass is float glass.

With the advent of trying to be energy efficient, most glass now has coatings that affect the solar radiation transmission through it. On the outside of the glass, much of the solar radiation is reflected back into the environment, adding to the solar radiation levels there. Of the solar radiation that passes through the glass, it is now modified and unnatural. This type of glass started to appear in the late 1980's. It can be made tinted or reflective to further improve the energy efficiency.

Double glazing became popular in the 1990's and most modern homes have it.

It is proven that the glass in your environment may be able to affect your health.

The correct way to understand how glass can affect your health is to refer to the research on sunscreens. Long term use of sunscreens are known to cause a toxic effect on the human body. If you use high factor sunscreen every day, you will eventually get sick. Glass functions just like high factor sunscreen, as it strips out the ultraviolet (UV) light that can burn you. You will find that it is difficult to get sunburn from sunlight that has passed through traditional glass window glazing. You have to spend significant time outdoors to get sunburned.

It is recommended that all glass on the inside of a building have coverings placed in front of it, such as nets, to prevent reflections and also to diffuse the modified spectrum solar radiation that passes through it. You should sit near to the windows when indoors, but not in the direct view of the Sun. You will get hot and fatigued in a direct view of the Sun. It is preferable to have the windows open whenever possible to let in the full spectrum of natural sunlight.

You may want to avoid spending extended time under windows and if you have a desk with a view, move it away from the window or reduce the solar radiation by using a window covering. You will most likely get solar radiation overload if you spend every day sitting with a direct view of the Sun.

On the outside of the building, it is recommended that plants be placed in front of the glass to absorb the reflected solar radiation. On a tall building, the windows should be covered with non-reflective downward facing louvers that prevent solar radiation reflections.

I have noticed that plants that are under smooth float glass windows show a doubled growth rate. They are reacting to the increased solar radiation levels and accelerated growth patterns are the result. The fact that the increased solar radiation does not kill them indicates that solar radiation levels in the past may have been much higher and the plants have genetics that have developed in much higher levels of radiation.

We are also seeing a much higher growth rate in children and it is being reported that they are going into puberty much earlier. This is likely related to the changing radiation levels that we are seeing take place around the world as the Industrial Revolution continues its acceleration.

Conservatories have become popular house additions and these are generally made out of glass. Again, use window coverings and plants to reduce the solar radiation levels in these types of glass buildings.

Double and triple glazing may pose a problem due to the following effects:

- Distortion of the glass.
- Chromatic aberrations.
- Coated energy saving glass.

The distorted glass occurs due to the slight vacuum that is present between the panes of glass. This may cause the reflected light to be lensed into a high powered beam of solar radiation. The power content of this may exceed that found in Space.

Chromatic aberrations may be an issue, due to the dispersion effect that it has on the spectrum of the light. This causes the light to be dispersed into the colors of the spectrum of the light and can be commonly seen on the surfaces where the light lands. It typically appears as a rainbow effect or a color at the edge of the light on the surface that it is cast on to.

Lead lights, window screens and dirt on the window pane may have the ability to cause diffraction and interference effects. It is unknown if any of these may be an issue to human health.

As you can see, we still have much to learn about the different types of glass and their interaction with human health.

The following pictures show how reflective double glazed glass can be and how it can randomly distort and focus light.

Light Forensics © Steven Magee

Double Glazed Windows

These three identical windows are at the entrance to my home.

Light Forensics © Steven Magee

Double Glazed Reflections

These are the reflections that the double glazed glass creates when the Sun is reflected from them. As you can see, each reflection is unique which indicates that each pane of glass has a different type of distortion.

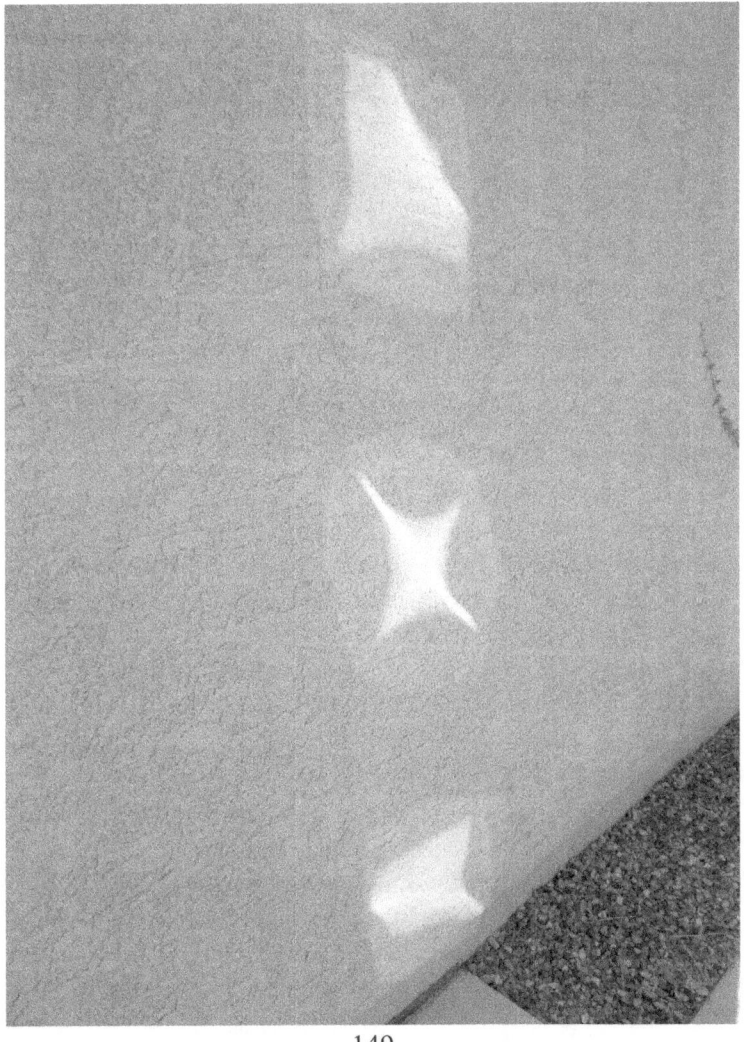

Clear ultra-violet (UV) transmitting acrylic window products are available and are commonly used by zoo's to prevent the animals becoming vitamin D deficient. It is recommended that you have these products installed where you spend the bulk of your daytime activities. This is especially important around developing children, as UV is known to be important in the correct development of children. Products that are specifically marketed for this purpose are "Monkey Shine" Solarcryl SUVT and LuciteLux Utran UVT. These are products that are commonly used in tanning beds and they have a high UV light transmission. You can easily obtain these products from tanning bed manufacturers and suppliers.

I have installed this in my office and my kitchen where I spend most of my day. My initial findings are that it has helped improve the final health problem that I am trying to eliminate, which is occasional fatigue. If you have developing babies and children, then you should install this in areas where they spend the bulk of their daytime. Full spectrum windows are particularly important for them. You do not need to install this in areas where you spend your evening and nighttime, such as bedrooms and bathrooms.

You should be aware that you can get sunburned through these products and that many things, such as plastics, may suffer from ultraviolet degradation. It is preferable to install UV transmitting glazing in areas that are shaded, such as the side of your home that faces the pole. In sunny locations, you should ensure that your window coverings can sufficiently reduce the sunlight levels to prevent you from getting sunburn!

Dr. John Nash Ott installed UV transmitting plastic windows in his home. This was due to noticing that his plants were not growing correctly indoors behind the glass windows. The UV transmitting products that he used improved the growth patterns. He also said that it improved his own health. He reported having better eyesight, thicker hair, far fewer incidences of colds and the flu, and excellent health after installing it. This famous statement summarizes his findings:

"Only a full spectrum of natural light could promote full health in plants, animals, and humans."

Dr John Nash Ott.

Privacy Glass

Privacy glass is commonly found in bathrooms and restrooms. It is glass that has patterns in it or has been intentionally produced with ripples in it. The problem with putting distortions into glass is that you affect how the light transmits through it.

Some light will pass through with relatively little change, whereas other light will be highly distorted. Around these types of windows you will generally find chromatic aberrations which will show up as colors on the edges of the bright patches of light that the window casts on the surrounding surfaces. Sometimes you will see rainbow effects with the glass spreading out the light into the color spectrum.

Bright and dark patches of light that textured windows create are a concern, as they can act like lenses and focus the light. These bright patches are high areas of solar radiation. Around windows that act like lenses you will commonly find areas of high solar radiation and their effects on human health are currently unknown.

The following pictures show the effects that these windows create.

"I have noticed that the solar radiation reflections from rippled privacy windows cause greatly accelerated growth patterns in plants"

Steven Magee

Light Forensics © Steven Magee

Heavily Textured Glass

This is the view through an acrylic block in my bathroom window. Note the heavy distortion in the image.

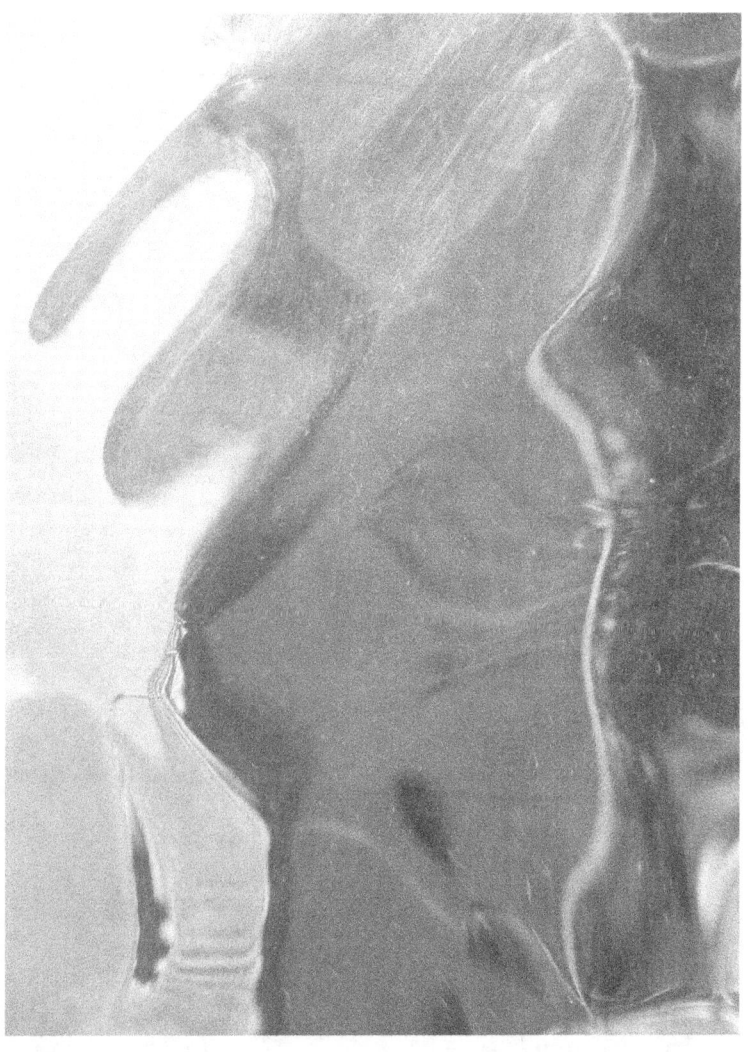

Chromatic Aberration

Chromatic aberration caused by the light transmission through the glass can make colors appear in the light that is cast onto surfaces. In this case, it created a rainbow effect.

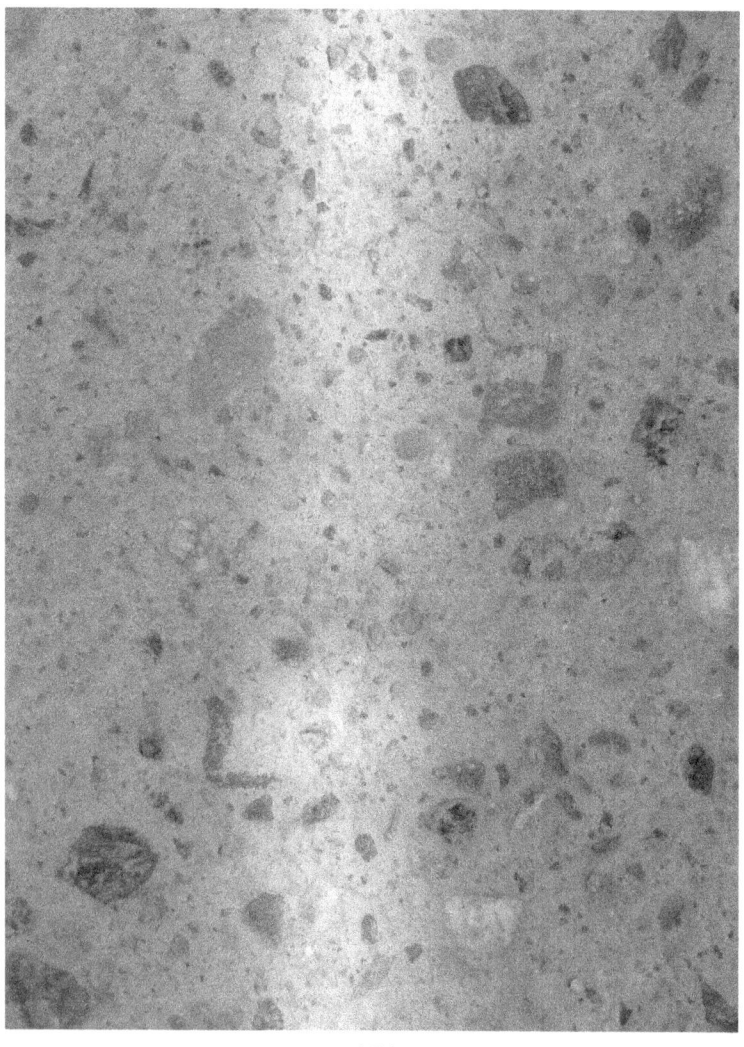

Chromatic Aberration

In this case the white light had a fringe of blue light at the top of the image that was caused by chromatic aberration.

Light Forensics © Steven Magee

Accelerated Growth

Sunlight reflecting from rippled windows greatly accelerates plant growth by up to three times normal rates.

Light Forensics © Steven Magee

Window Coatings

Anything unnatural that filters the broad spectrum of solar radiation will create an artificial and possibly toxic environment for humans.

Glass coatings modify the solar radiation spectrum on both the outside and inside of the glass. Many of these coatings cannot be seen by the human eye and the glass will appear to be transparent to visible light. The glass may be highly reflective to other wavelengths such as ultraviolet (UV), infrared (IR) or radio frequencies (RF).

The atmosphere when mixed with pollution is just like a window coating. If you fill the atmosphere with toxins, then you really cannot be surprised if the solar radiation transmission through it becomes toxic to humans.

Sunscreens act like window coatings and modify the solar radiation received by the body. You should avoid the use of sunscreens, as they can be toxic to the body if used daily. The man-made chemicals may also have an ability to poison the body in the long term.

The following pictures are of coated double glazed glass.

"Better keep yourself clean and bright; you are the window through which you must see the world."
George Bernard Shaw

Light Forensics © Steven Magee

<u>Sun Refection in Double Glazed Glass</u>

This is how the Sun looked when reflected from the double glazed pane of glass. There were three reflections of the Sun!

Light Forensics © Steven Magee

Wall Reflection

And this was the reflection from it onto the wall. Note the bright patches of solar radiation that are actually higher in power than that of Space!

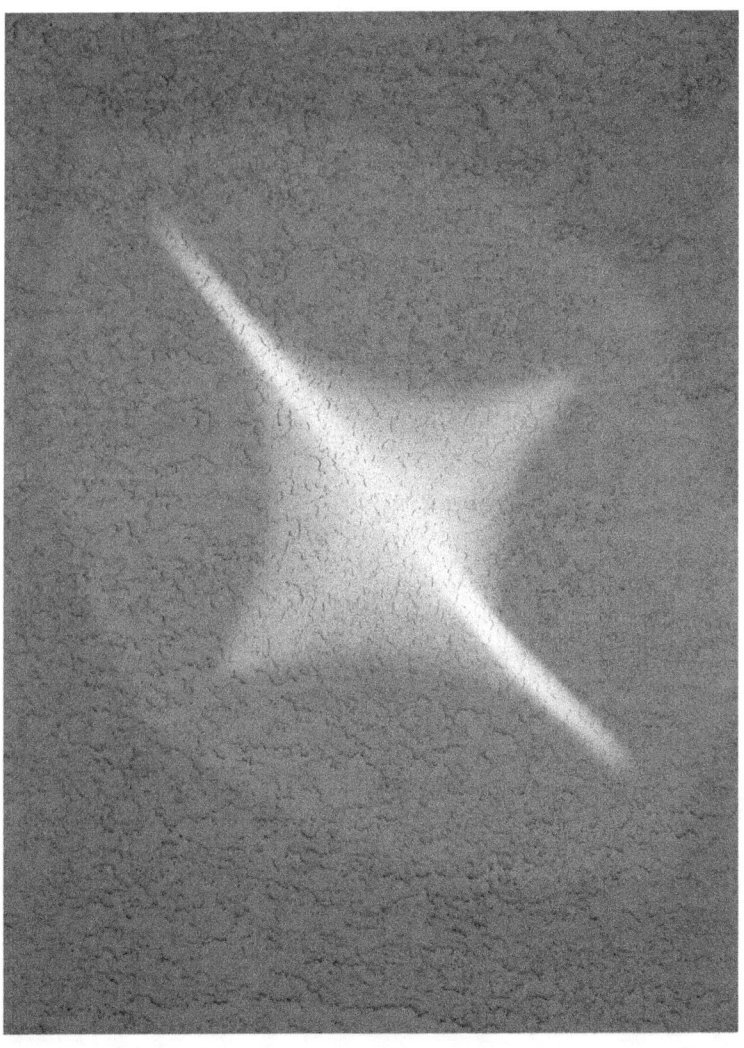

Roofs

Roofs that can be seen from the ground can reflect solar radiation to the ground and increase the solar radiation levels.

It is recommended that roofs that can be seen from the ground have trees placed near to them to reduce the solar radiation reflections that they create.

Roofs that absorb solar radiation will act like heaters and radiate their heat into the surrounding air. In a city environment, there are many buildings that will be heating the surrounding air and raising the city temperature.

Multiple houses that are situated on curves may act like lenses. They have the potential for the solar radiation that is reflected from their pitched roofs to combine and significantly raise the solar radiation levels around them. This is a concern to humans who may pass through these high solar radiation environments.

It is plausible that the roof on your home may be able to affect your health.

"How prone poor Humanity is to dam up the minutest remnants of its freedom, and build an artificial roof to prevent it looking up to the clear blue sky."
E. T. A. Hoffmann

Homes Focusing Radiation

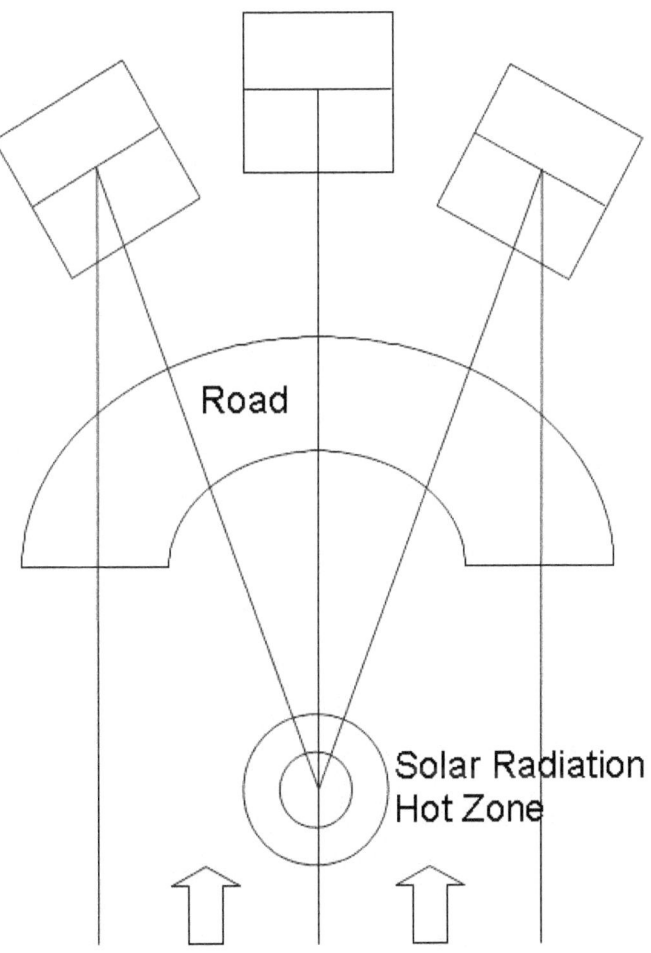

Air Conditioning

Air conditioners remove heat from the interior of buildings. This heat is formed by the absorption of solar radiation and hot outside air temperatures by the building. Air conditioners work by using energy to transfer the heat energy from the inside of the building to the outside. They essentially work by dumping large amounts of heat and energy into the outside air and raise the outside temperature. This may cause shimmering of the sunlight. It sounds a lot like global warming.

Air conditioning has allowed humans to live almost anywhere in the world. Without it, many population centers would not exist. Unfortunately, it has increased energy consumption significantly and a corresponding release of fossil fuel exhaust emissions into the atmosphere. Future human population increases should be focused on areas that have stable climates that do not require the use of air conditioners.

"The peculiar malaise of our day is air-conditioned unhappiness, the staleness and stuffiness of machine-made routine."

Eugene B. Borowitz

Paints

Modern paints have been developed that are highly reflective. These work by reflecting solar radiation that hits the paint back into the environment. This is undesirable from a human perspective as it raises the solar radiation levels around the building or structure.

It is plausible that the solar radiation that is reflected from the paint on the outside of your home may be able to affect your health.

Outdoor paints should be developed that reflect very low levels of solar radiation. It is suggested that they should mimic nature and have the same reflected solar radiation spectrum as trees and flowers. Gloss paints should be avoided and paints should have low levels of reflectivity.

On the inside of the home, you should paint it in light natural colors. Your nighttime lighting will fill your home with the reflected colors from your paints. Bright colors that are associated with atmospheric pollution filtering effects such as yellows, oranges, and reds should be avoided. I would recommend that you keep to whites and light cream colors. The brighter your home is, the less electric lighting that you will need to use of a nighttime. It is also healthier.

"Live in rooms full of light."
Cornelius Celsus

Ground Materials

Solar radiation can be reflected up from the ground. The level of the reflection is dependent on the material that the ground is made of. A dry and smooth concrete sidewalk generally will reflect about 55% of the solar radiation back into the environment. It will have a modified solar radiation spectrum to match the material that reflected it.

The power of the reflection increases the closer you are to it, as such, the feet, ankles and knees are most vulnerable to these types of solar radiation reflections.

You should avoid using smooth man-made materials for ground cover. Instead, use rough natural materials such as wood or dark stone.

It is proven that ground materials may be able to affect your health.

"Keep your eyes on the stars, and your feet on the ground."
Theodore Roosevelt

Architecture

The multiple-Sun reflections do not seem to appear in nature. I have spent many weeks looking for them in the National Parks of the USA and failed to locate the multiple-Sun effect. The National Parks are as close to a natural environment that you will find in the USA.

Nature creates scattered, filtered, polarized, diffracted and interference sunlight at much lower power levels. This averages out to much lower irradiance values compared to those of the cities. There must be a reason why nature does this and it would be foolish to ignore nature.

Nature is in harmony with the Sun. We must look to nature and follow its guidance. Nature reflects light by scattering and creating low power levels. We should do the same in our societies.

We are supposed to receive the light that nature creates. Light from trees and grass has beneficial effects on human health. Just ask any camper how they feel when they are camping in a natural environment. Generally they will tell you that they love the clean air. What they were not aware of is that the light is also very different in nature and they are experiencing beneficial effects from this as well.

How can we mimic nature? Here are a few suggestions:

- Use rough surfaces throughout.
- Use natural building materials such as rough stone and wood.
- Use dark colors that absorb light.
- Use colors that reflect light with the same color spectrums that are found in nature.

- Sidewalks and roads should be made from rougher, less reflective materials.
- Create shade wherever possible.
- Plant more trees and create a natural environment.
- Reflect only scattered light.
- Shade reflective surfaces with non-reflective downward facing louvers.
- Use flat roofs that can not be seen from the ground.
- Limit the height of the buildings to below that of the tree canopy.
- Keep to single story construction if possible.
- Illuminate the building with natural sunlight.

Architecture should be designed by architects who are trained in optics. They must understand the reflective effects of their construction materials. A good understanding of albedo is a must.

Engineers must understand that buildings and construction materials create parallel, semi-parallel, and non-parallel reflections, polarization, diffraction and interference effects, modified solar radiation and high levels of albedo, and they will need to factor that into their particular engineering field.

Human health in a multiple-Sun environment needs to be evaluated and understood by the medical profession. The long term effects of continual high irradiance exposure and modified solar radiation are currently unknown.

We are still constructing mirrored buildings. Perhaps it is time to take a break and examine the human solar radiation environment before committing to any more mirrored buildings?

"A doctor can bury his mistakes, but an architect can only advise his clients to plant vines."

Frank Lloyd Wright

Light Forensics © Steven Magee

Homes

The arrangement of homes can create concentrated solar radiation reflections from them. Multiple homes that are arranged in a curved formation can act like a lens and focus the solar radiation reflected from them into the surrounding area.

If you are feeling ill frequently, you should assess the solar radiation environment that the homes in your area create to rule this out. Pay close attention to headaches, nausea, and intestinal pains.

Multiple people dying before the age of sixty may be an indication of problems in a street. Look for the following history in residents:

- Brain tumors.
- Strokes.
- Brain and spinal cord problems.
- Mental issues.
- Nerve issues.
- Heart attacks.
- Cancer.
- Learning difficulties in the young.
- General health problems.

It is proven that your neighborhood may be able to affect your health.

Haunted houses may have their root cause in an unnatural electromagnetic radiation environment. This may show up as the people living there having strange dreams. An unnatural radiation environment may well cause hallucinations, giving the sensation of the house being haunted! It is interesting to note that ghost hunters use the same equipment as environmental engineers.

When purchasing a home it is recommended that you assess the electromagnetic radiation environment of both the home and the surrounding area.

"We suffer primarily not from our vices or our weaknesses, but from our illusions. We are haunted, not by reality, but by those images we have put in their place."
Daniel J. Boorstin

Light Forensics © Steven Magee

Home Selection

Here are some hints and tips for selecting natural electromagnetic radiation homes:

- Avoid homes that:
    - Are on curves in the road due to lensing effects that reflections from multiple homes may create.
    - Are painted in light reflective colors.
    - Have smooth exterior walls.
    - Have lots of glass.
    - Have glass windows that change the color of the light.
    - Have pitched roofs that can be seen from the ground.
    - Are paved with modern reflective construction materials.
    - Are overlooked by taller structures.
    - Have views of the roofs of the surrounding homes.
    - Have streetlights nearby.
    - Are near built up areas, especially industrial zones.
    - Are near to utility equipment.
    - Are near to transmitter systems.
    - Have radiation transmitting utility meters.
    - Are devoid of natural wildlife.
    - Have no trees or vegetation.

- Look for homes that:
    - Are surrounded by trees.

- Have plenty of vegetation.
- Have lots of shade.
- Are covered in climbing plants.
- In a natural setting.
- Are single story only.
- Are old and have aged.
- Are made of natural rough materials such as wood and dark stone.
- Are painted in dark non-reflective colors on the outside.
- Have the majority of windows facing the pole.
- Have "full spectrum" acrylic windows installed.
- Have window coverings on both the inside and outside of the home.
- Have bedrooms facing the pole.
- Have underground utilities.
- Have plenty of distance between the neighboring properties in all directions, preferably several hundred feet.
- Have housing associations that have banned wireless products and amateur radio operators.

For information on healthy buildings, the free film "First Earth" at http://www.davidsheen.com/firstearth/film.htm provides excellent advice.

The following pictures demonstrate the solar radiation reflections that buildings can create.

"Nature is my manifestation of God. I go to nature every day for inspiration in the day's work. I follow in building the principles which nature has used in its domain."

Frank Lloyd Wright

Light Forensics © Steven Magee

Street Solar Radiation

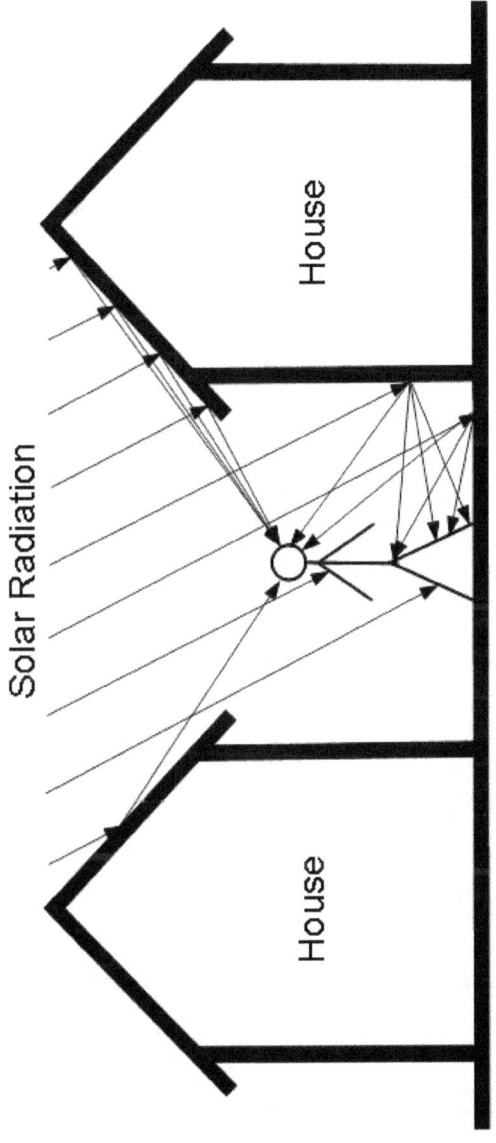

Home Solar Reflections

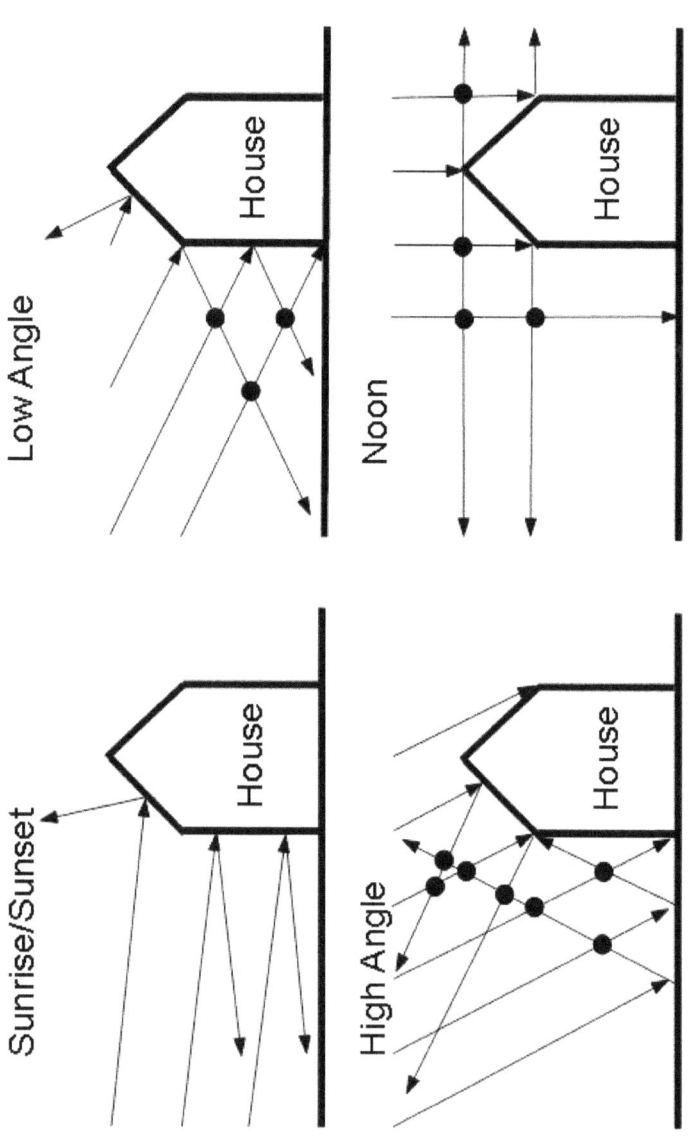

Cars

The prolific adoption of cars and transport systems has been rapid over the last few decades. Cars and transportation systems can be highly reflective. This increases the solar radiation levels in the environment.

Cars in particular create horizontal solar radiation reflections. You should keep them in the shade or in a garage to prevent this. The face, neck, chest and reproduction areas are especially vulnerable to these solar radiation reflections, due to them being horizontal.

Nighttime car headlights use a wide variety of lighting technologies and some of these are more toxic than others. Some of the newer car headlights are affecting the night vision of the oncoming drivers! The indicators and brake lights are now commonly light emitting diodes (LED) and the long term health effects of these is still in the process of emerging.

Cars also dump heat and exhaust gasses into their environment.

These effects are undesirable and humans should start to develop transportation systems that are either underground or shielded from view by vegetation and trees. Humans should move away from regular car commuting to and from work and into local working that is within walking distance.

It is proven that cars can affect your health.

The "Multiple-Sun" effect that cars create is shown in the next picture.

"Road rage is the expression of the amateur sociopath in all of us, cured by running into a professional."

Robert Brault

Light Forensics © Steven Magee

"Multiple-Sun" Effect in Cars

The "Multiple-Sun" effect occurs in cars and raises the radiation environment to unnaturally high levels.

Light Forensics © Steven Magee

Artificial Light

Artificial light sources are a concern as the light is different from sunlight. So you are worried about artificial lighting and are thinking that you can fix it by using full spectrum lighting products? Think again. While full spectrum lighting products sound appealing, the truth is that there is no such thing as full spectrum artificial lighting. It is a marketing ploy.

What full spectrum really means is that the light is as close to the Sun's spectrum as can be possibly made using current technology. Unfortunately it is not sunlight and never will be. The sunlight spectrum is constantly changing during the daytime and with the seasons. It changes with the latitude also.

All types of artificial lighting have the possibility of making you ill. Artificial lighting should be avoided if your health is important to you.

If you are going to have artificial lighting in your environment, then it should have a plant in front of it so that the light becomes modified by the plant. This is shown on the next page.

Light Forensics © Steven Magee

Light Modification by Plants

Here is the "Star of Bethlehem" as produced by a halogen lamp and a plant

Light Forensics © Steven Magee

Color temperatures can be used to specify light sources. Here is a list of the color temperatures in Kelvin of modern light sources, as listed on Wikipedia:

- *1,700K Match flame.*
- *1,850K Candle flame, sunset/sunrise.*
- *2,700–3,300K Incandescent light bulb.*
- *3,350K Studio "CP" light.*
- *3,400K Studio lamps, photofloods, etc.*
- *4,100K Moonlight, xenon arc lamp.*
- *5,000K Horizon daylight.*
- *5,500–6,000K Vertical daylight, electronic flash.*
- *6,500K Daylight, overcast.*
- *9,300K CRT screen.*

As can be seen, the color temperature varies between the different sources and also the different times of the day.

The Color Rendering Index, or CRI for short, is similar to the color temperature. Wikipedia says the *"Color rendering index, or CRI, is a measure of the quality of color light, devised by the International Commission on Illumination (CIE). It generally ranges from zero for a source like a low-pressure sodium vapor lamp, which is monochromatic, to one hundred, for a source like an incandescent light bulb, which emits essentially blackbody radiation. It is related to color temperature, in that the CRI measures for a pair of light sources can only be compared if they have the same color temperature. A standard "cool white" fluorescent lamp will have a CRI near 62."*

The color temperature and CRI do not give the full picture. You also need to be aware of the radiation spectrum. Unfortunately, most gas discharge lamps have a spiked radiation spectrum that does not occur in nature. Due to this, you should avoid any artificial lighting that is created from gas discharge sources, such as mercury vapor, fluorescent, sodium, and so on.

Mercury based lighting mystifies me. We know that mercury is toxic to humans. So why would we make lighting products with it? In the future, mercury lighting products may be proven to be harmful to human health.

Stage lighting is known to affect some performers. Looking at bright stage lights for extended periods may eventually cause damage to the eye. This may eventually result in light sensitivity that is known as "Photophobia".

The next page shows how the florescent (mercury) and tungsten (traditional) light bulb spectrums compare.

Florescent Spectrum

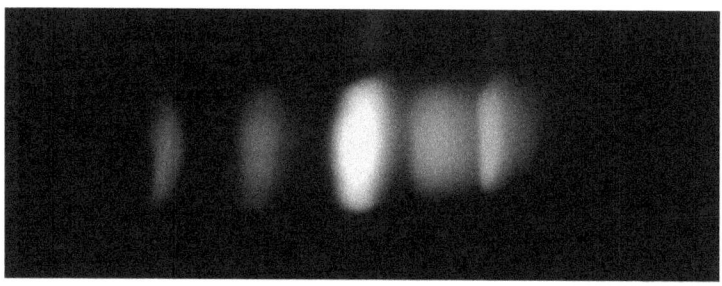

Note that the spectral lines are not continuous, but rather broken up. This is typical of gas discharge lighting. It does not occur in nature.

Tungsten Spectrum

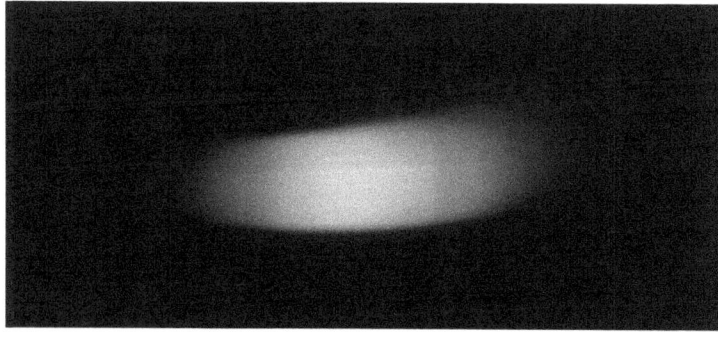

A smooth continuous spectrum that is typical of what nature produces.

A simple way of gauging the indoor daytime light environment for the human is to do a light test. Turn off your indoor lighting in the middle of the day. Note how bright the surroundings are. Now turn on your indoor lights and see if it is brighter. If the indoor environment is brighter then it means that you need to have more natural light coming in to your daytime areas. You can do this by adding more windows or skylights.

You should be aiming to illuminate your indoor daytime environment with natural outdoor light, not electrical lighting products. This light should be full spectrum natural light that the intensity can be controlled with window shades. Working in daytime environments that are illuminated with artificial lighting products is undesirable for human health.

If you work in a daytime indoor environment, then the lighting should mimic what nature does. It should have a natural daytime spectrum of light that matches sunlight. This would be achieved with filament lights that have the correct amount of blue and ultraviolet light in their spectrums to mimic outdoor daylight. Your indoor lighting level should be approximately 1,000 lux.

From 10:00 – 14:00 there should be an additional set of lights that is turned on that increases the brightness of the office environment, to mimic the peak in sunlight that occurs outdoors. The indoor environment during this time should have an illumination level of approximately 2,000 lux. You can easily achieve this in your office environment by simply having a desk lamp that you switch on during that time to increase the light illumination that you are exposed to. You should be using filament light bulbs of the correct spectral emissions for this exposure.

You should make sure that you go outdoors for an hour at solar noon and sit in the shade of trees. Do not wear any sunglasses, glasses, contacts, or sunscreen for this exposure. You need this exposure daily to keep up the solar cycle in the human body. Without it, you may start to get fatigued as the day goes on. Daily outdoor exposure to sunlight is very important if you have an indoor occupation.

If you do not get the correct light exposures in the day, then your sleep cycle may kick in. The human body when kept in an indoor environment of low lux light will not realize that it is daytime, as it cannot sense the increasing levels of sunlight that the genetics are accustomed to. As such, by late morning your body may start sending a signal for you to sleep!

If you can, during any of your daily breaks, you should try and go outdoors to get natural sunlight. You will also be getting fresh air and pollen exposure, which are also necessary for good health.

The recommended cycle for indoor daytime lighting is shown on the next page.

Indoor Daytime Lighting Cycle for Human Health

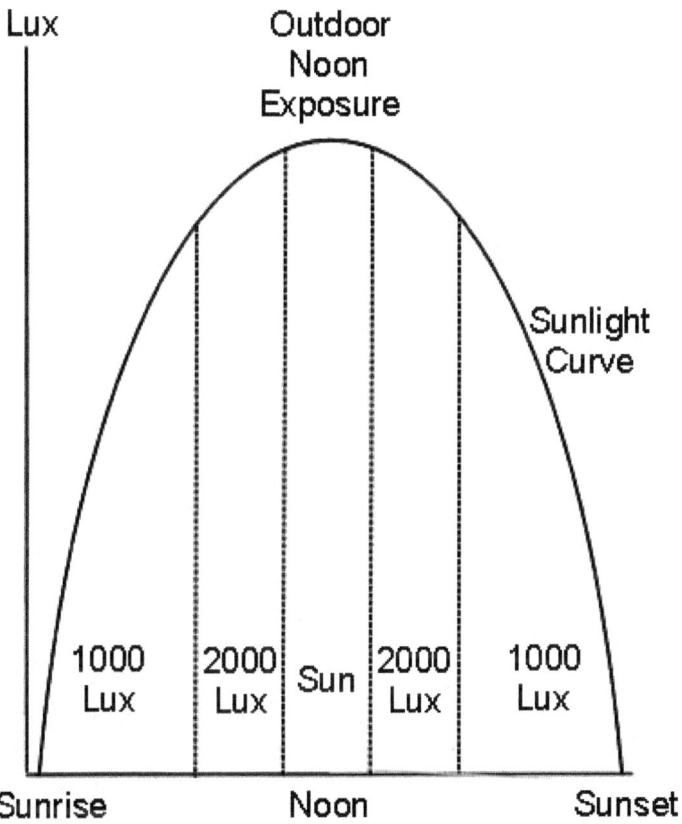

Light Forensics © Steven Magee

Nighttime lighting is very different from daytime lighting. You want to be using products that have minimal blue light in them. Blue light exposure is well known to cause insomnia. If you install lighting products that have too much blue light in their spectrums, then you may enter into a life of insomnia and not realize that it is your light bulbs that are causing it! Insomnia rapidly leads to fatigue and onto depression. These daytime lighting products are commonly sold as "Daylight" or "Full Spectrum" light bulbs and should not be used in nighttime applications.

You should stick to the tried and tested filament light bulbs for your nighttime exposures. Avoid the compact florescent (CFL) and LED bulbs as some of these are well known for their excessive blue light content. Keep your lights low, as bright light can also trigger insomnia.

Most people do not actually realize it, but they are polluting the interior of their homes with nighttime electric lighting. This pollution has become quite severe in the last few decades with the adoption of compact florescent lights (CFL) and light emitting diode (LED) products. These products typically have unnatural spectrums of light and can have a wide range of electromagnetic radiation emissions from them. Some of them give out too much blue light and this may induce insomnia and macular degeneration of the eye. They can turn the home wiring into a radio transmitter which may lead to radio wave sickness in the human.

I currently advise people to use filament bulbs. I presently use conventional filament light bulbs for nighttime lighting at my home. Low voltage halogen lighting products should be avoided due to the emissions from them. They may have high amounts of ultraviolet light, create dirty electricity, and electric and magnetic fields. I keep the lighting low and just sufficient for what I am doing. You will not find any electronic lamp dimmers in my home, as they are a product that you should avoid using. Lamp dimmers can create dirty electricity, and electric and magnetic fields.

You should also be using the correct voltage light bulb. In the USA these are sold as either 120 volt or 130 volt light bulbs. You should be using the 120 volt versions, as they are far more efficient at producing light. The 130 volt versions should only be used if your light bulbs are frequently breaking within a few days of installing them. If you use 130 volt light bulbs when they are not needed, your light bulbs will last a very long time, but will give out a poor quality of light.

You should be aware that the many sources of artificial lighting can affect your mental and physical health. You should be choosing your daytime artificial lighting products based on the proven health benefits of "Full Spectrum" light bulbs that are comparable to outdoor daylight. Health benefits have been reported by many gardeners who use these products to grow their plants during the winter months. Nighttime artificial lighting products are different to daytime products and should be used in your home for good sleep patterns.

"Full spectrum lights should be used in all daytime offices."
Steven Magee

Tanning Lamps & Beds

Tanning lamps and beds are popular. There are no doubts that they can improve peoples health and how they look. People who use tanning beds appropriately can be seen to radiate energy, they look great! However, get it wrong and you may be in trouble. An ultraviolet radiation burn, premature aging, or disease may end up being the result.

Tanning beds are unusual in the fact that people lay right next to florescent tubes! You could not pay me money to do that today. I have used a tanning bed in the past as my family owned one. I only used it a few times and I remember feeling great afterwords. The surge in ultraviolet radiation exposure on the human cellular system was wonderful.

I am older and wiser and I would not lay next to florescent tubes. There are some very strange things going on around florescent tubes regarding electromagnetic fields and emissions from them. Electrical current is flowing through the tubes and your body is very close to that current flow. The tubes will have frequencies of electrical energy running through them that will unnaturally couple into the human body. Extended exposure to this may make you sick and it could affect your mental functioning. Dr. John Nash Ott found biologically harmful emissions from the tube ends that were deforming plants.

The light that they emit is pulsating, generally at a high frequency. The spectrum of light cannot be found in nature. Florescent tubes generally have large spikes of specific frequencies of light and are lacking frequencies of light in other areas.

Tanning lamps are a little bit better, as you do not lay on them but rather sit in front of them. There is some distance between you and the electromagnetic radiation emissions which helps. They still have the light spectrum problems that the tanning beds have. A variant of the tanning lamp is the Seasonal

Affective Disorder (SAD) lamp that is used to treat winter depression.

So you want a tan and do not want the risks of tanning beds and tanning lamps? I can recommend the installation of ultraviolet transmitting "Full Spectrum" acrylic windows in the appropriate areas of your home. You will get a nice color simply by sitting next to the window daily! Of course, the people to buy the acrylic from are the tanning bed suppliers and manufacturers. It is the same as what they use in their products. People who have SAD should have shady full spectrum windows and sit facing them daily.

"For excellent health and a good skin color, I recommend that people sit next to a shady ultraviolet transmitting window when indoors"

Steven Magee

Light Forensics © Steven Magee

Television, Computers & Phones

Televisions, computer displays and mobile phones are all sources of artificial light. You should be wary of your exposure to these as they may be able to impact your health.

The recent adoption of large screen televisions may bring with it an increase in human health problems in the future. People watching three dimensional images frequently may be an issue in the long term. Both of these could possibly be like a ticking time bomb. It is recommended that if you have a display in your environment that you keep it as small as possible. You may want to experiment with the brightness and contrast controls to get it to emit the lowest amount of light and still be comfortable to use. It is advised that your screen should not dominate your field of view.

For television producers, you should avoid producing evening programs with lots of blue in their images. Evening programs should be using warm colors that avoid the insomnia causing blue light exposures.

Children who get addicted to video games have been documented as having the following problems:

- Depression.
- Anxiety.
- Social phobias.
- Lower grades.

The problems that displays can cause appears to be documented as computer vision syndrome (CVS). Computer vision syndrome (CVS) is a temporary condition resulting from focusing the eyes on a display for protracted, uninterrupted periods of time. People who wear glasses and contact lenses appear to have the highest frequency of this condition.

Some symptoms of CVS include:

- Headaches.
- Blurred vision.
- Neck pain.
- Redness in the eyes.
- Fatigue.
- Disruption of the circadian cycle.
- Eye strain.
- Dry, irritated eyes.
- Double vision.
- Polyopia.
- Difficulty refocusing the eyes.

It is now emerging that computers and televisions are actually causing changes in the physical structures of the brain. You should limit your time in front of these devices and take frequent breaks from them. It is preferable to sit as far away from them as you can. You should discourage children from sitting close to these devices as they can have very strange electromagnetic emissions from them. Many of these emissions have been proven to be biologically harmful.

Use your display in an environment that has good lighting in it and plenty of plants. Your display should not be the brightest thing in your environment.

Computers should have their screen designs to be largely a black background with white writing to enable the display to emit the lowest amount of radiation and to give high contrast. Computer anti-glare and security filters may be an issue also.

Displays are linked to insomnia and you should avoid using these items during the evening. If you are having insomnia issues, you should stop using items with displays and see if it clears up. If it does, you will know that the display was causing your problems.

To prevent these issues you should not use screens in low light environments. You should be using them in natural daylight environments. During my research into human health, I realized that you need to have your computer screen placed with an outdoor view behind it. This is because the human mind and body is supposed to receive full spectrum outdoor light during the daytime. Many people have their computers in cubicles or against walls that provide the eye with no natural light whatsoever. It appears for this reason that they suffer from fatigue during the day. If your computer that you use in the daytime has no outside view behind it, then I would suggest that it is in your interest to move it to an area that does.

The next picture shows the correct alignment of a computer screen and outdoor light. It is preferable to have this arrangement with a window that does not have a direct view of the Sun during the daytime. If your window does have a direct view of the Sun, use an outdoor shade or trees to block it. It is also preferable to use your computer next to a window that is made out of full spectrum ultraviolet transmitting acrylic.

"Television has changed a child from an irresistible force to an immovable object."

Unknown

Computer Screen Alignment

The correct alignment of a computer screen to the shaded full spectrum ultraviolet transmitting acrylic window.

Cinema Light

Movie theater projectors have been constantly changing over the years. Today they are commonly Digital Light Projection (DLP) systems. The light is typically provided by a high-pressure mercury-vapor metal halide arc lamp or a xenon arc lamp.

There appears to be two standards of cinema projectors and these are:

- 2K (2048×1080) at either 24 or 48 frames per second.
- 4K (4096×2160) at 24 frames per second.

Watching a movie in a dark theater on a very large screen is an interesting dynamic for the human mind and body to cope with. While I was researching this book, I had noticed the following occurring after visits to the cinema:

- Insomnia.
- Fatigue.
- Headaches.
- A change in mental state.

Typically, these symptoms would last up to three days after watching the movie. There is a very strange dynamic to movie theater light today. This may extend into the surround sound systems also, as strange sound frequencies are also known to interfere with the biological system. Having noticed that these symptoms typically follow a trip to the cinema, I now tend to avoid the movies.

I call this health effect: "Cinema Hangover"

"Photography is truth. The cinema is truth twenty-four times per second."

Jean-Luc Godard

VR Displays & Microscopes

During the development of virtual reality (VR) displays it was noted that they were giving rise to severe vision problems and nausea. The newer eye-glass displays may produce vergence issues, where the eyes start to lose their ability to work together.

People who are working full time with microscopes are reporting problems with their health also. The National Board of Occupational Safety and Health in Sweden report, titled "Investigation of Visual Strain Experience by Microscope Operators at an Electronics Plant", concludes that 80% of microscope operators had visual strain. A statistically verified relationship was found to exist between visual eye strain and uncorrected astigmatism, poor eye coordination and time spent at the microscope.

Feeding the eyes with separate images and artificial light appears to cause problems and these effects may apply to three dimensional televisions in the future. Further study of these effects is desirable before three dimensional products become widespread.

"Most people are awaiting Virtual Reality; I'm awaiting virtuous reality."

Eli Khamarov

Light Forensics © Steven Magee

Strobe Lights

Strobe lights are found in many applications:

- Emergency vehicles.
- Road works.
- Lighthouses.
- Antenna system night lights.
- Tall structure aircraft warning lights.
- Camera flash guns.
- Rotational test equipment.
- Lightning.

Strobe lights are a problem because they emit an electromagnetic radiation pulse. This pulse of energy can be very intense up close. It is not just light energy that is emitted, but energy across the spectrum of electromagnetic radiation. It is a good idea if you work with this type of lighting to limit your exposure to it. It is preferable to avoid it completely if you can.

The toxicity to wildlife of strobe lights was noticed by the operators of lighthouses. They have a tendency to confuse the wildlife that can see them.

Strobe lights can cause strange growth patterns in plants. The high intensity flashes and the strange electromagnetic pulses are the cause of these strange growth patterns. The effect has been studied in humans and it can trigger epilepsy.

Lightning is a particularly impressive strobe light. Up close, the electromagnetic pulse (EMP) can be very large. There are many electromagnetic emissions associated with lightning and they can travel a long way.

Light Forensics © Steven Magee

"Electricity is really just organized lightning."
George Carlin

Light Forensics © Steven Magee

Flicker Light

Some lighting products suffer from flicker that is not noticeable to the eye. The newer LED lights and gas discharge lights appear to suffer from this effect. Indeed, most streetlights are actually flashing at 120 times per second. It is simply too fast for your eyes to detect it.

Flicker can do a lot of very strange things to the human mind and body. Commonly reported effects are:

- Epilepsy.
- Headaches.
- Disorientation.
- Anxiety.
- Seizures.
- Motion sickness.
- Eyestrain.

The health problems of flicker generally peak in the 5-30 times per second range. As such, you should not spend time in environments that have flashing or flickering lights. This may a problem for emergency service workers who work in environments that have these strobe lighting products in them. When multiple emergency vehicles are together, then their light flash rate will be much higher and may cause these problems to occur. The electromagnetic pulses from strobe lights may lead to radio wave sickness to occur in people who are close to them.

Flicker fusion is the name given to the speed above which the eye perceives continuous light as opposed to flashing light. It occurs above 15 flashes per second.

"I have seen vast, perhaps unbelievable, changes during the journey that has brought me from the flicker of a lamp in a small Bengal village to the chandeliers of Delhi."

Pranab Mukherjee

New Lighting

I would recommend that you avoid the use of the new lighting that has been developed, such as gas discharge, compact florescent (CFL) and light emitting diode (LED) lighting. These have been developed in order to use less energy at the expense of the quality of the light.

High intensity discharge (HID) lamps have appeared in projector televisions, public areas, warehouses, supermarkets, movie theaters, football stadiums, roads, parking lots and car headlamps. In cars, they have a blue appearance and have started to cause problems with other drivers due to their high intensity.

Ultra high performance high intensity discharge (UHP-HID) lamps that can be found in projector TV's may be a problem if they break as they contain mercury. This could be an issue in an enclosed space such as a house due to the mercury vapor that would be released into the air.

All artificial lighting should be generated by heat. This is how the Sun generates light. Unfortunately, there are no filament lighting products that can generate the same temperature as the midday Sun. As such, all filament lighting products are a compromise in the daytime application.

"We now know a thousand ways not to build a light bulb"
Thomas Alva Edison

Light Forensics © Steven Magee

Streetlights

The streetlights that are present in modern society are polluting the view of the night sky and in most cities, it is barely visible. This may be a problem as it may interact with the eyes and the skin to cause unwanted effects in the body. It most likely will interfere with the circadian rhythm that governs the sleep cycle. Circadian problems are linked to:

- Insomnia.
- Fatigue.
- Depression.
- Cardiovascular disease.
- Cancer.
- Aggression.
- Mistakes at work.

It is interesting to note that some diseases appear to be following the progress of electricity and nighttime lighting. Indeed, I have noticed a trend in premature deaths in the people that I know and the presence of streetlights outside of their homes. If you have a streetlight outside of your home, I would recommend that you install blackout blinds on the bedrooms that the light shines into. The light that streetlights create is very unnatural.

During the development of the book "Toxic Electricity" I was conducting an artificial lighting test that I had to stop which involved lighting products that are typically used in streetlight applications. These were a compact florescent lamp (CFL), a light emitting diode (LED) lamp, and a high pressure sodium lamp.

During two weeks of running the experiment, extreme fatigue showed up and all I wanted to do was sleep day and night. I turned off the experiment and the fatigue cleared up. All three Dieffenbachia (Dumb Cane) plants went on to show deformities. Within a year the plant that was grown under the sodium light was dead. It may be a case of "Delayed Radiation Complications" that are known to occur from six months to many years after the initial radiation exposure.

This matches my observations that something biologically strange is going on near to sodium street lights. This appears to be currently documented as "Street Light Interference" and is documented in the book "SLIDERS: The Enigma of Streetlight Interference" by Hilary Evans.

Street lighting products typically generate electrical system harmonics, emit strange spectrums of light, flash at 120 hertz, and may emit unnatural forms of electromagnetic radiation. If you are not feeling well and you live near to streetlights, you may want to electromagnetically screen the side of the home that faces the streetlights, in case they are giving off biologically harmful electromagnetic emissions.

Dr. John Nash Ott called street lights "Crime Lights", as he had noticed that crime rates were higher in areas that had them. This effect has been noticed by other researchers as well. Most streetlights are providing average illumination in the range of 3 to 17 lux with much higher levels directly under the streetlight. A full moon is about 0.3 lux, so the streetlight is far brighter. You need to be careful with exposure to streetlights for this reason, as the strange light that they emit will be interfering with your nighttime biological systems.

If you live near to streetlights, then you would be wise to get familiar with the type of lighting products in use and the known health problems associated with those particular products. You should monitor the health of your family to see if they are displaying any health issues that may be caused by the streetlights. It is a bad idea to let children play out in the dark under these unnatural lights and the stray voltage effects in the street may be higher during the nighttime. You should discourage your children from sitting on the ground under streetlights for this reason. The stray voltage exposure risk is far greater when it is wet. I lived in a home in the past that had a sodium streetlight outside it and I now associate that home with poor health and relationship problems.

There are a number of definitions associated with nighttime lighting:

- Glare is created by light that shines horizontally.
- Sky glow is the bright halo over cities at night.
- Light trespass is light from one property spilling into another adjacent property.
- Over-illumination is light that is far above what is needed for the activity.

The International Dark Sky association can provide more details: http://www.darksky.org/

Research on many types of wildlife shows that light pollution can alter behaviors, foraging areas, and breeding cycles. The book "Ecological Consequences of Artificial Night Time Lighting" has more information on the subject.

The nighttime city view of San Diego is shown on the next page. The following picture shows the potentially biologically harmful emissions of streetlights.

"When we speak about the quality of light and its importance to the well being of all living organisms, the contributions of Dr. John Ott stand out above those of other researchers in the field."

Dr. Jacob Liberman

Light Forensics © Steven Magee

San Diego Streetlights

The streetlights make it look like a weird color of daytime.

Streetlight Emissions

Streetlights have many sources of biologically harmful emissions associated with them.

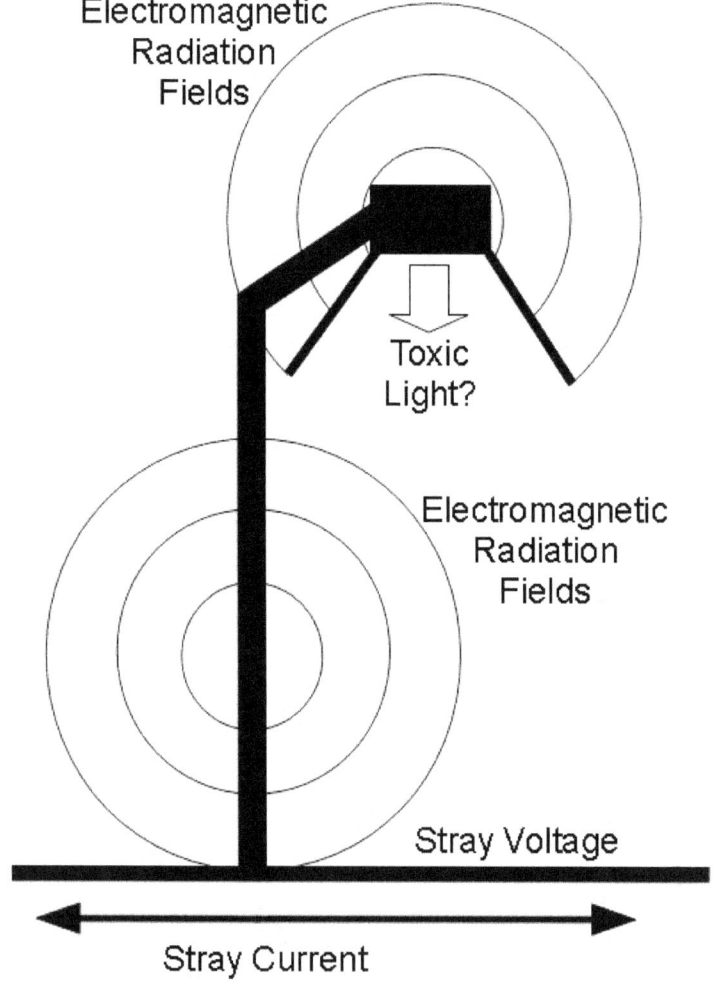

Light Forensics © Steven Magee

Gaslights and Flares

Gas flares are one of the most biologically toxic forms of light around. You will typically see these around:

- Refineries.
- Sewer plants.
- Chemical plants.
- Landfills.
- Oil and gas drilling operations.

For many animals, they are lethal; flying animals are attracted by the light and fly into it! Some of the flaring releases radioactive particles into the environment and these will be blown downwind of the flare. All flares release pollution into the environment and you do not want to be downwind from this pollution. As we know from studying volcanic pollution, these clouds of pollution can travel hundreds of miles before they fully disperse into the environment. I would recommend that you do not live nor work near to flaring activities.

This was a problem in the era of gas lighting, as the homes and workplaces would fill up with carbon monoxide! Fortunately, the drafty homes and workplaces back then would allow a circulation of fresh air into the area to offset the pollution. Gas lights were not in use for long before electric lighting took over from them. A nice feature of gas lighting is the absence of high speed flicker problems. If you film a gas light at high speed, it gives out a constant light with no evidence of flashing.

"Even in your home, nobody dies of smoke inhalation, they die of carbon monoxide."

Geoffrey Winters

Arc Welding

Arc welding produces a very high powered light from the electrical arc. In welders, it generally causes a sunburn reaction. "Arc Eye" (Photokeratitis) is a condition associated with welders and is the reason why you see them using face shields. You should never watch a welder working, otherwise you may develop arc eye.

Arc welders are a group of people who get extensive exposure to stray voltage and electromagnetic radiation emissions. It is likely that the majority of arc welders have some form of radio wave sickness. The arc gives off many forms of electromagnetic emissions.

It is a bad idea to live near to a person who operates an arc welder, as they will be injecting strange frequencies of energy into the electrical and grounding (earthing) systems. They will also fill the area with radio wave emissions. They really should be banned from residential communities where developing children are present.

"What is to give light must endure burning."
Viktor Frankl

Bedroom Light

Bedroom light is probably one of the most important forms of light. The best form of bedroom light is no light. You should be concerned when you open your eyes in the middle of the night and can see things. Your bedroom should be completely dark while you sleep. You should not be able to see anything!

Things that should not be in your bedroom are:

- Night lights.
- LED clocks.
- Cell phones.
- Wireless products.
- Electricity.
- Products that glow.

Your bedroom is where you go to biologically regenerate. It must be completely dark for this process to work well. It is undesirable to have electricity in the room and electrical products as they may interfere with the regeneration process. If you have light coming into the room, then you should purchase black out blinds to prevent it. You should regard your bedroom as a refuge of darkness where you recharge for the next day of light. Simply Yin and Yang.

"In order for the light to shine so brightly, the darkness must be present."
Francis Bacon

Food Spoilage by Light

Supermarkets have known for a long time that light may cause food to spoil. In particular, supermarkets have realized that artificial lighting can accelerate the spoiling of fresh food. The next time you are in the supermarket, take a look at the lighting in the fresh food section, it may well be different to that in the rest of the store. As such, they have identified lighting products that do not age the fresh food as quickly.

Spoilage of food by light is called photo-degeneration and it can cause problems with:

- Pigments.
- Vitamin levels.
- Fats.
- Proteins.

The density of the food will determine the depth of the photo-degeneration and liquids appear to be the most affected by it. Photo-degeneration can result in:

- Discoloration.
- Off flavor.
- Nutrient losses.

Factors in photo-degeneration are:

- Light source strength.
- Type of light.

- Distance from the light source.
- Length of exposure.
- Optical properties of the packing materials.
- Optical properties of the food.
- Oxygen concentration of the food.
- Temperature.

The aging effect of light on food may have a similar effect in humans. Food packaging should be opaque to light to prevent the photo-aging effects that may occur while the food is waiting to be sold.

"Research has shown that even small amounts of processed food alter the chemical balance in our brain and cause negative mood swings along with noticeable dips in energy."

Marilu Henner

Light Forensics © Steven Magee

Colors & Moods

It has been known for a long time that colors can affect your mood. Now that the sunsets have turned orange and red, let us see what these colors produce in the human:

- Orange: Daring, stimulating.
- Red: Stimulating, excitement, anger.

It is recommended that you stay indoors during the time of the sunrise and sunsets. Watching the sky at this time may have health implications, particularly so in polluted areas.

In locations that are nearer to the poles the Sun does not rise above the horizon very far. At these locations, there is a high level of atmospheric filtration taking place on the solar radiation during the daytime. Given the levels of pollution in the atmosphere, daytime may be bad for human health due to this level of filtration.

Good colors are:

- Yellow: Cheerful, positive.
- Green: Calming.
- Blue: Soothing.
- Brown: Warm.

Bad colors are:

- Red: Anger.
- Violet: Rare in nature, regarded as artificial.

Light Forensics © Steven Magee

- Black: Depressing, tired.

Arranged in the color spectrum, we get:

- Infrared: Heat.
- Red: Stimulating, excitement, anger.
- Orange: Daring, stimulating.
- Yellow: Positive.
- Green: Calming.
- Blue: Soothing.
- Indigo: Deep contemplation.
- Violet: Unnatural, rarely occurs.
- Ultraviolet: Burns and damages skin.

Looking at the color spectrum, we see that the center appears healthy while the outer limits appear unhealthy.

Full spectrum light is that which contains all of the colors as nature put them together. This is commonly referred to as white light. White is symbolic of purity and cleanliness. The opposite to this is black or no light. Black is often associated with evil and death and is the color of fossil fuels.

Man-made lights that are used at nighttime are not natural. As such, nighttime lighting should be kept as low as possible so that the human body does not absorb too much of it. In artificial lighting environments it is advisable to use plants to modify the light to a natural form of light. The reflected light from plants may be essential to good human health.

"Green is the prime color of the world, and that from which its loveliness arises."

Pedro Calderon de la Barca

Light Forensics © Steven Magee

Aggression

Humans have already started to figure out that nature is essential to good human health, as this United States Department of Agriculture article demonstrates: "Do Trees Strengthen Urban Communities, Reduce Domestic Violence?" By W. C. Sullivan, Ph.D. & Frances E. Kuo, Ph.D.

Cities are characterized by a whole host of social ills-- from anonymity, to incivility, to outright violence--that are strikingly less prevalent in rural areas. Why is this? The physical environment a person lives in has profound effects on their social behavior. Social psychologists have shown that people in cities behave differently from people in rural areas in part because they live in crowded, noisy places, or in places that lack open space. But cities differ from rural areas in another important way as well--rural areas have something that's often lacking in urban areas--nature. Can part of the unsociableness of city dwellers be traced to the lack of plants in their everyday surroundings?

With support from the National Urban Community Forestry Advisory Council, we set out to answer these questions in one of the grimmest of urban settings--public housing in a major city.

As these pictures show, the number of trees immediately outside each of the 28 buildings at Robert Taylor Homes in Chicago vary considerably. Some buildings are surrounded only by concrete and asphalt, while others have trees, grass, and even flowers. Using aerial photographs and on-site analyses we chose 10 buildings with trees and 8 buildings without trees. We then interviewed 75 African-American women living in those buildings about their social behavior and compared the answers from women living in different buildings.

While the amount of plant life varies from building to building, very little else does. The buildings are architecturally identical. There are no systematic differences in the groups of people living in one building or another, perhaps because residents have very little choice in the specific apartment they are assigned. This gives us some confidence that differences we find in social behavior of people living in buildings with and without trees are really due to the trees--not differences in crowding, noise levels, or availability of open space, not differences in race, economic status, or even nature preferences in the people living there.

Do people who live in buildings with trees get along and treat each other better than people living in buildings without trees? The results of these interviews are not only interesting; they also provide new arguments in support of urban forest programs. Let's look at some of the highlights.

DO TREES STRENGTHEN URBAN COMMUNITIES?

For some time there have been stories about community gardens revitalizing inner city urban neighborhoods (Francis, Cashdan & Paxson 1984; Lewis 1972, 1979). Until now, however, no one has systematically examined the effect of trees on relations among neighbors.

We are finding signs of stronger communities where there are trees. In buildings with trees, people report significantly better relations with their neighbors. In buildings without trees, people report having fewer visitors and knowing fewer people in the building. In buildings with trees, people report a stronger feeling of unity and cohesion with their neighbors; they like where they are living more and they feel safer than residents who have few trees around them.

Why might trees contribute to better relations among neighbors? In 100 observations of outdoor common spaces in two public housing developments, we are finding that outdoor spaces with trees are used significantly more often than identical spaces without trees. We suspect that in urban areas, trees create outdoor spaces that attract people. When people are drawn to spaces with trees, they are more likely to see and interact with their neighbors, more likely to get to know each other and become friends.

Stronger ties among neighbors may be a good thing, but it becomes an even more convincing reason to support urban forests when you consider what neighborhood ties mean for residents' functioning. There is evidence that people with strong neighborhood ties are more physically healthy (Cassel 1976; Cobb 1976), more mentally healthy (Gottlieb 1983), less likely to neglect or abuse their children (Garbarino & Sherman 1980), and less likely to rely on costly social services in times of need (Biegel 1994; Gottlieb 1983; Collins & Pancoast 1976). In other words, these findings suggest that by investing in urban forests, a city might reap such dividends as a lowered incidence of child abuse, and decreased demand on social services.

DO TREES REDUCE VIOLENCE?

Two studies have shown a connection between trees and lower levels of violence (Mooney & Nicell 1992; Rice & Remy, in press). But these studies involved prison inmates, and Alzheimer patients living in nursing homes. What about people who are not living in institutional settings?

We are finding less violence in urban public housing where there are trees. Residents from buildings with trees report using more constructive, less violent ways of dealing with conflict in their homes. They report using reasoning more often in conflicts with their children, and they report significantly less use of severe violence. And in conflicts with their partners, they report less use of physical violence than do residents living in buildings without trees.

Why might trees contribute to less violence in the home? Imagine feeling irritated, impulsive, about ready to snap due to the difficulties of living in severe poverty. Having neighbors who you can call on for support means you have an alternative way of dealing with your frustrations other than striking out against someone. Places with nature and trees may provide settings in which relationships grow stronger and violence is reduced.

WHAT DOES THIS MEAN FOR URBAN FORESTRY?

In times of tight budgets, public officials look to reduce costs, and in doing so it is reasonable that they eliminate amenities. Trees have often been considered amenities. But what if urban foresters could report to city officials that trees help lower social service budgets, decrease police calls for domestic violence, strengthen urban communities, and decrease the incidence of child abuse in a city? Would the urban forest be considered an amenity then?

In this study, we are finding that urban forests help build stronger communities, and in doing so, they contribute to lower levels of domestic violence. Although no strong conclusions can be made from a single study, these findings are encouraging and exciting. At a time when the nation's attention is focused on issues such as crime prevention, health care, and the plight of single mothers, these findings suggest that trees can help address some of the most important problems in society today. We believe that urban forests are not mere amenities--that they are a basic part of the infrastructure of any city, as necessary as streets, sewers, and electricity.

REFERENCES

- *Biegel, D.E. (1994). Help seeking and receiving in urban ethnic neighborhoods: strategies for empowerment. Prevention in Human Services. 3 (2-3): 119-143.*

- *Cassel, J. 1976. The contribution of the social environment to host resistance. American Journal of Epidemiology. 104(2): 107-123.*

- *Cobb, S. 1976. Social support as a moderator of life stress. Psychosomatic Medicine. 38(5): 300-314.*

- *Collins, A.H.; Pancoast, D.L. 1976. Natural helping networks: a strategy for prevention. Washington, DC: National Association of Social Workers.*

- *Francis, M.; Cashdan, L.; Paxson, L. 1984. Community open spaces: greening neighborhoods through community action and land conservation. Washington, DC: Island Press.*

- *Garbarino, J.; Sherman, D.1980. High-risk neighborhoods and high-risk families: the human ecology of child maltreatment. Child Development, 51(1): 188-198.*
- *Gottlieb, B.H. 1983. Social support as a focus for integrative research in psychology. American Psychologist. 38(3). 278-285.*
- *Lewis, C.A. 1972. Public housing gardens: landscapes for the soul. In Landscape for Living. Washington DC: United States Department of Agriculture Yearbook of Agriculture.*
- *Leuis, C.A. 1979. The sprouting of the inner city. Psychology Today. 13(1): 12-13.*
- *Mooney, P.; Nicell, P.L. 1992. The importance of exterior environment for Alzheimer residents: effective care and risk management. Gestion des soins de sante. Health Care Management forum: 5(2): 23-29.*
- *Rice, J.S.; Remy; L.L. (in press). Cultivating self development in urban jail inmates. Journal of Offender Rehabilitation.*

Copies of this article and many others on human health and its relation to the trees can be obtained from the Landscape and Human Health Laboratory at the University of Illinois: http://lhhl.illinois.edu/

"One of the most tragic things I know about human nature is that all of us tend to put off living. We are all dreaming of some magical rose garden over the horizon instead of enjoying the roses that are blooming outside our windows today."

Dale Carnegie

Light Modulation

Up until now we have been talking about the many forms of light that are present around us. Some of you by now will have realized that what we are taking about is light modulation. Modulation basically means that the Space solar radiation is altered by the many variables on its way to the ground. We can say that the radiation is modulated by the many environmental variables that it is subjected to.

Modulated solar radiation can do many strange things to biological organisms:

- Accelerated growth patterns.
- Retarded growth patterns.
- Dormant growth patterns.
- Biological patterns go out of synchronization with nature.
- Burn.
- Alter mental functioning.
- Cause aggression.

Producing artificial light sources creates modulated light, as non of the artificial light sources today are comparable to daylight.

As we have seen, you need to be very careful with how you allow radiation to be modulated. The various forms of modulation of radiation can affect the human. We need to be very careful with how we allow sunlight to be modulated due to this.

"The law of conservation rigidly excludes both creation and annihilation. Waves may change to ripples, and ripples to waves,—magnitude may be substituted for number, and number for magnitude,—asteroids may aggregate to suns, suns may resolve themselves into florae and faunae, and florae and faunae melt in air,—the flux of power is eternally the same. It rolls in music through the ages, and all terrestrial energy,—the manifestations of life, as well as the display of phenomena, are but the modulations of its rhythm."

John Tyndall

Natural Light

So what functions are the trees performing that when they are not present will cause people to become aggressive?

The solar radiation interference effect that the tree canopy makes when solar radiation passes through it is probably the answer. This effect is called "Tree Canopy Light Interference". Light interference is a very big area of research in the optical and astronomical communities currently, it just has never been applied to the tree canopy.

Light is made up of waves and these waves can interfere with each other when passed through multiple apertures. The tree canopy makes many apertures that create the light interference effect. The result of this is that the solar radiation under the tree canopy is very different from the solar radiation above it. It is as different as night is to day.

Trees absorb the majority of the solar radiation and only reflect a small percentage of it back into the environment. They also change the color temperature and spectrum of the solar radiation. To sum up, here are the effects that the tree canopy has on solar radiation:

- Filtering of solar radiation.
- Polarization of solar radiation.
- Diffraction of solar radiation.
- Interference of solar radiation.
- Significant reduction in the power level of solar radiation.
- Create a stable power level of solar radiation.
- Color temperature modification of solar radiation.
- Spectrum modification of solar radiation.

- Conversion of solar radiation into natural energy.

Without the tree canopy reducing and modifying the solar radiation, humans are subjected to flicker. This is an effect that is happening at sub-second speeds that is not noticed by the human eye. However, a high speed camera that shoots several frames per second can see this occurring. The Sun is basically increasing and decreasing its intensity due to atmospheric distortions and interference. Astronomers know this effect as "Astronomical Seeing". This effect may be able to induce dizziness, fatigue, headaches, epilepsy and nausea. Modern flicker may be a consequence of atmospheric pollution and may be far more severe than in the past.

An effect that is similar to this is broken clouds passing in front of the Sun. These produce extreme power cycles in the solar radiation levels. The power levels can change by over 90% very quickly. The human body appears to have problems with this high level of frequent power cycling and again may experience dizziness, fatigue, headaches, epilepsy and nausea.

Solar radiation is made up of direct, diffuse and albedo radiation power levels. Direct is the view of the Suns disk, diffuse is the sky in general (the blue and cloudy part) and albedo is the reflections. Of these, direct contains over 90% of the energy and diffuse contains under 10%. There is no limit on the level that the reflections can be at and in a modern environment, such as a city, the albedo can increase the power levels many times of the sky based solar radiation of direct and diffuse combined.

You only realize that you have light problems when you contrast your light sources to outdoor daylight. This is shown in the next picture. The following picture shows the interference light rings from the tree canopy.

"Show me your garden and I shall tell you what you are."
Alfred Austin

Light Quality

Indoor light filtered by four panes of coated low-E glass on the left as contrasted to natural sunlight through an open window on the right. The center line is shade from the frame.

Light Forensics © Steven Magee

<u>Airy Disk Diffraction by Trees</u>

The trees appear to produce the "Circle of Life" from diffraction and interference effects.

Light Forensics © Steven Magee

Lighting Levels

So what is a healthy level of lighting? If we take a look at the forest environment, then the answer is obvious. Keep lighting levels low and use plants in front of artificial lights to create light interference. The forest has an illumination level of about 2,000 lux during the daytime. As such you should aim for a daytime lighting level of 2,000 lux in order to be healthy. This is generally found near to windows. Use natural plants in front of your lights and windows to create light interference.

As for nighttime lighting, you should think candles! Not necessarily use candles, but rather the illumination level that candles create. There is a reason why candles are considered romantic and it is likely related to the low level of light that they create.

Nighttime over-illumination is a problem in the modern world and it is proven to affect your health. Keep it as low as possible and only increase lighting levels if you feel that you need more light in your environment. Avoid bright lights and lights with a lot of blue light in them of a nighttime. Blue light exposure may give you insomnia. Filament light bulbs are recommended for their lack of blue light.

If you have your environment too bright during the nighttime, then you may upset the circadian rhythm that governs your sleep cycles. Keep lighting as low as possible during the nighttime. You should also keep your skin covered as much as possible to prevent it from absorbing the artificial light.

Incorrect radiation levels may be able to affect your sex drive and it may be proven in the future that human sex drive is governed more by radiation types and levels than any other factor, even more so than hormones!

"Humans make thousands of units of vitamin D within minutes of whole body exposure to sunlight. From what we know of nature, it is unlikely such a system evolved by chance."

Dr. John Cannell

Light Forensics © Steven Magee

Summary

The human appears to be an outdoor forest animal by genetics that has decided to be an indoor animal. Unfortunately, this does not appear to match its genetics and the indoor society appears to be making people ill in large numbers.

The human mind and body is greatly affected by the various forms of light exposures. Incorrect light exposure can induce strange thought patterns and affect your ability to process information. Long term incorrect light exposure should be expected to lead to significant health problems that may not be able to be reversed. I find it concerning that very few people in modern society have the correct light exposures needed for good health.

To be in good health, you should spend your day either outdoors or next to a shady window with a green natural view. If next to a window, then that window should be an ultraviolet transmitting "Full Spectrum" acrylic window. The outdoors should be in your field of view during the day so that your eyes can sense the changing daylight levels. When working indoors, you should take frequent breaks outdoors to get true outdoor daylight exposure. A little direct Sun is a good thing, but do not overdo it.

The eyes appear to circulate the entire volume of the blood through them approximately every two hours. It is important that the blood is irradiated by outdoor daylight for proper biological functioning of the human cellular system. You need to make it your top priority that this occurs daily. Paying attention to this will help prevent you from being placed onto prescription medications in the future.

As individuals, we can control our own natural environments. Our homes should be under the tree canopy. Windows should have plants next to them on both the inside and outside. The gardens of our homes should be like forests. The inside of our homes should be filled with plants. The outside of our homes should be dark, non-reflective natural colors. Our work environments should be filled with plants and natural lighting. The top thing that you can do to stay in good health or improve your health is to surround yourself with plant life and natural daylight. This includes eating live plant foods such as organic salads, raw vegetables and fruits.

A natural green environment has been shown to improve mental health, increase self discipline and impulse control. Less access to nature is related to increased attention deficit and hyperactivity disorder symptoms, higher rates of anxiety disorders, and higher rates of clinical depression.

Direct beam solar radiation, a direct view of the Sun, contains over ninety percent of the solar radiation energy that is received at ground level. We must block this direct view with trees that convert the energy naturally. This will result in a cooler ground level environment that is conducive to good health in humans with the best light nutrient.

Trees are solar radiation absorbers and suppressors and we must start replanting native trees, especially so in the human environments. The schools would be a good place to start so that the solar radiation levels around the young are reduced back to natural levels. Reducing the solar radiation levels may allow the human body to repair any damage that may have occurred from exposures to high levels of it.

Humanity needs to be in the presence of a tree canopy in order to be a peaceful race. The trees appear to prevent us from developing illness and disease, the trees have a lot of power over us. As such, we need to spend time evaluating the relationship of the natural environment to that of a modern man-made environment.

Climate change is very real and has the potential to lead to human extinction. It is now reasonable to state that climate change has progressed into Earth change. The Earth appears to be entering a period of unrest that has not been observed in recent centuries.

Light Forensics © Steven Magee

The sky being filled with excessive water vapor and pollution is having impacts on life around the world. We know that natural solar radiation is critical to correct development and life. We also know that unnatural solar radiation is harmful to development and life. Continued pollution of the atmosphere will eventually be catastrophic to all life on this Earth.

It appears that clouds may have the ability to trigger evolution by modulating the solar radiation transmission from Space to the ground. It is likely that we entered a new period of human evolution some time ago, given that the clouds appear to have changed their structure. We are alive during a time of great change on the Earth. How we will be remembered by future generations will be based on the decisions that we make in the coming years.

As individuals, we can control the direction of the human race. It is recommended that you ensure that the leaders of the nations have the natural world and human health at the top of their agenda's. Use your vote wisely, your children's future is at stake. We are the masters of our children's future. It is recommended that the children voice their desires for the future to their parents.

Be healthy by being outdoors in the natural daylight with nature!

I can recommend the book "Toxic Health" for those who want to understand the many aspects that go into being healthy. "Toxic Electricity" details the many known detrimental aspects of the electrical system that can affect your health. "Solar Radiation, Global Warming, and Human Disease" discusses how the rapidly changing environmental conditions that are associated with the modern corporate world may lead to rapid increases in human disease in the next fifty years.

I hope that you enjoyed the book and I wish you the best of health.

"Light is the basic component from which all life originates, evolves, and is energized. Light and health are inseparable."

Ken Ceder

Light Forensics © Steven Magee

Definitions

Sunlight

- Sun: Our closest star, a giant nuclear reactor in the sky.
- Natural Sunburn: Sunburn from the Sun and reflections from nature.
- Man-Made Sunburn: Sunburn from the Sun and a mix of natural and man-made reflections and optical effects.
- Full Spectrum: Sunlight that contains the full ultraviolet, optical and infrared spectrum as it occurs in nature at sea level.
- Direct: Light that occurs in the sky where the view of the Sun's disk is.
- Diffuse: Light that occurs across the rest of the sky, excluding the Sun's disk.
- Albedo: Light that occurs by reflections from objects.

Multiple-Sun Effect

- Multiple-Sun: Two or more Sun's are present.
- Stereo-Sun: Two Sun's are present that are opposite each other.
- Surround-Sun: Three or more Sun's are present around you.
- Light-maze: A grouping of glass covered buildings that sunlight bounces around in.
- Lighthouse: A reflected Sun that follows you as you move around the building.

Light Forensics © Steven Magee

Light

- Parallel Light: Light that travels in parallel.
- Semi-Parallel Light: Light that travels in a similar direction with some scattering present.
- Non-Parallel Light: Scattered light with no bright areas.
- Filtered Light: Light that has reduced its power level and may have lost parts of the full spectrum.
- Reflected Light: Light that has been reflected from a surface and has taken on the spectral properties of that surface.
- Polarized Light: A type of light that can occur by filtration or reflection which causes polarity.
- Chromatic Aberration: Occurs when light passes through a medium and starts to exhibit fringes of color.
- Diffraction: Occurs when parallel light passes over an object which causes the light waves to start spreading outwards.
- Interference: Occurs when spreading light waves start to cross with each other and interact.
- Glare: Created by light that shines horizontally.

Streetlights

- Sky Glow: The bright halo over cities at night.
- Light Trespass: Light from one property spilling into another adjacent property.
- Over-Illumination: Light that is far above what is needed for the activity.

"The stars are the street lights of eternity."
Unknown

Light Forensics © Steven Magee

References

- Adam Ant
- Albert Einstein
- Alexander Graham Bell
- Alfred Austin
- A.L. Tchijevsky
- Antyllus
- Aretaeus
- Arnold Schwarzenegger
- Barbara Minton
- Bell Hooks
- Benjamin Franklin
- Bible
- Bill Gates
- Camilla Rees, MBA
- Center for Disease Control and Prevention. www.cdc.gov
- Christopher Shays
- Clea Duvall
- "Color and Light: Their Effects on Plants, Animals and People." book by Dr. John Nash Ott.
- Confucius
- Cornelius Celsus
- Dale Carnegie
- Daniel J. Boorstin

- David Suzuki
- Deepak Chopra
- Denise Linn
- Dennis Weaver
- Desiderius Erasmus
- Dr. Abraham Hoffer
- Dr. Frank Apperly
- Dr. John Cannell
- Dr. Maki Takota
- Dr. Michael F. Holick
- Dr. William Davis
- Duane Graveline MD MPH
- Do Trees Strengthen Urban Communities, Reduce Domestic Violence? Paper by By W. C. Sullivan, Ph.D. & Frances E. Kuo, Ph.D.
- "Ecological Consequences of Artificial Night Lighting" book by Catherine Rich and Travis Longcore.
- Eli Khamarov
- E. T. A. Hoffmann
- Eugene B. Borowitz
- "Exploring the Spectrum: The Effects of Natural and Artificial Light on Living Organisms." film by Dr. John Nash Ott.
- Francis Bacon
- Frank Lloyd Wright
- Galileo Galilei
- Geoffrey Winters

Light Forensics © Steven Magee

- George Bernard Shaw
- George Carlin
- Gloria Steinem
- Google Maps: http://maps.google.com/
- Gunther Grass
- "Health and Light: The Extraordinary Study That Shows How Light Affects Your Health and Emotional Well Being." book by Dr. John Nash Ott.
- Herbert Hoover
- Herodotus
- Hippocrates
- Ignazio Silon
- "Investigation of Visual Strain Experience by Microscope Operators at an Electronics Plant." Paper by Occupational Safety and Health, Sweden
- James Buchan
- James Thurber
- Jean-Luc Godard
- Jean Toomer
- John Lubbock
- John Maher
- John Tyndall
- John William Strutt
- Ken Ceder
- Kevin Kelly
- Khalil Gibran
- Leif Grunseth
- Les Brown

- "Light Medicine of the Future" book by Jacob Liberman, O.D., Ph.D.
- "Light, Radiation, and You: How to Stay Healthy." book by Dr. John Nash Ott.
- Lombardi Comprehensive Cancer Center: http://lombardi.georgetown.edu/
- Louis Pasteur
- Marilu Henner
- Michael Fish
- Mike Adams
- "My Ivory Cellar; [the story of time-lapse photography]." book by Dr. John Nash Ott.
- Napoleon Bonaparte
- NASA: http://www.nasa.gov/
- National Renewable Energy Laboratories www.nrel.gov
- N.P. Willis
- Ornette Coleman
- Paracelsus
- Pedro Calderon de la Barca
- Plato
- Polly Toynbee
- Pranab Mukherjee
- Professor d'Arsonval
- Ralph Waldo Emerson
- Robert Brault
- Robert Southey
- Sir Noel Peirce Coward

- Theodore Roosevelt
- Thomas Alva Edison
- Thomas Berry
- "The Wind Farm Scam" book by John Etherington.
- Tony Haffer
- Uri Geller
- Vandana Shiva
- Vincent Van Gogh
- Viktor Frankl
- William Wordsworth
- "Wind Turbine Syndrome" book by Nina Pierpont, MD, PhD.
- Wikipedia http://www.wikipedia.org/

"None of us is as smart as all of us"
Unknown

Internet

Manufactures of ultraviolet (UV) transmitting full spectrum acrylic window glazing sheets are:

Lucite International, Inc: LuciteLux UTRAN UVT:
http://www.lucitelux.com/product.aspx?productID=4

Spartech: Solacryl "Monkey-Shine" SUVT:
http://www.spartech.com/polycast/Spartech-Polycast-Solacryl-Monkey-Shine.pdf

Vitamin D Wiki is a useful collection of vitamin D information:
http://vitamindwiki.com/VitaminDWiki

"The Internet is becoming the town square for the global village of tomorrow."
Bill Gates

Acknowledgments

This book was influenced by:

- Claudia Sandoval MSW for her wisdom on how trees and nature interact with human social behaviors.
- My neighbors for their understanding and assistance with my biological experiments.
- Dr. John Nash Ott for his extensive research into health, light, and radiation. His lasting legacy of publications was a wonderful gift to the next generation:
    - My Ivory Cellar; [The Story of Time-Lapse Photography].
    - Health and Light: The Extraordinary Study That Shows How Light Affects Your Health and Emotional Well Being.
    - Light, Radiation, and You: How to Stay Healthy.
    - Color and Light: Their Effects on Plants, Animals and People.
    - Exploring the Spectrum: The Effects of Natural and Artificial Light on Living Organisms.
- The numerous people who are in the reference and internet chapters that have worked diligently to bring the important science of environmental health to the masses.

"Help others achieve their dreams and you will achieve yours."
Les Brown

Light Forensics © Steven Magee

About the Author

Steven started his career at one of the largest university research and teaching hospitals in Europe. Working in the electrical engineering group, he obtained a Bachelors with Honors in Electrical and Electronic Engineering. Human health was a strong draw and he moved into the biomedical team, serving the regions hospitals. During this time he developed a fascination for human illness and disease and the causes of it, many of which were not understood.

He joined the Isaac Newton Group of Telescopes in 1999 and went to live in La Palma. La Palma is part of the Canary Islands, governed by Spain. During this time he worked with the leading European astronomers and developed his astronomical and optics skills. He became fluent in Spanish and their culture.

In 2001 he became a Chartered Electrical Engineer and joined the W. M. Keck Observatory in Hawaii. This was the world's leading astronomical facility and home to the world's two largest segmented mirror telescopes. Steven developed segmented optics and interferometry skills while working alongside world leading astronomers. During this time Steven constructed his own off-grid solar powered home in the last of the traditional Hawaiian fishing villages in Miloli'i, Hawaii. He learned Hawaiian Pidgin English and the Hawaiian culture during his time there.

In 2006, Steven became the Director of the MDM Observatory in Sells, Arizona, USA. Working for Columbia University and later, Dartmouth College, he developed the facility to modern standards. He learned an appreciation of the native Americans and their culture from the Tohono O'odham Nation.

In 2008, Steven joined the solar power revolution that was sweeping the USA and commissioned the largest CIGS thin film solar photovoltaic installation in the world.

A year later he commissioned the largest solar photovoltaic power plant in the USA. The system rated power was quoted as 25,000,000 watts AC with over 90,500 solar modules that were mounted to 158 single-axis tracker systems in three hundred acres of land.

He went on to develop the solar photovoltaic team for a large international company.

In 2010 he started to research radiation and publish the leading books on the subject.

"All truths are easy to understand once they are discovered; the point is to discover them."
Galileo Galilei

Light Forensics © Steven Magee

Author Contact

I hope that you found the book informative and please let me know about any questions or comments about the book. I can be contacted through the StevenMageeBooks channel on www.youtube.com.

I am a consultant in the areas that I research at Environmental Radiation LLC and please feel free to contact me for any help or assistance. This is the website:

http://www.environmentalradiation.com/

You can follow the twitter feed at:

Steven Magee @EnvironmentEMR

The Facebook page is:

https://www.facebook.com/EnvironmentEMR

You may find my other books useful:

Solar Photovoltaic

- **Complete Solar Photovoltaics for Residential, Commercial, and Utility Systems:** Steven Magee has combined his three top selling books on solar power systems into one edition. Complete Solar Photovoltaics will train you on solar photovoltaics and show you how to design grid connected solar photovoltaic power systems. Operations and maintenance is detailed to enable you to have a complete understanding of solar photovoltaics from start to finish.
- **Solar Photovoltaics for Consumers, Utilities, and Investors:** This book details solar photovoltaic systems for consumers, utilities and investors. This would encompass residential, commercial and utility systems

that are connected to the utility grid. There is a discussion of the different technologies available for the consumer and their advantages and disadvantages. For the utilities, there is invaluable advice on planning and constructing large projects. For the investor, forward looking statements try to predict the future of solar photovoltaics.

- **Solar Photovoltaic Training for Residential, Commercial, and Utility Systems:** This book details solar photovoltaic training for those who are interested in this area and also for those who are already working in the field. This would encompass residential, commercial, and utility systems that are connected to the utility grid. It is a comprehensive overview of a rapidly growing world of solar photovoltaic power generation technology.

- **Solar Photovoltaic Design for Residential, Commercial, and Utility Systems:** This book details how to design reliable solar photovoltaic power generation systems from a residential system, progressing to a commercial system, and finishing at the largest utility power generation systems. By following the guidelines in this book and your local solar photovoltaic electrical codes, you will be able to design trouble free solar power systems that give many years of reliable operation. When designed well, solar photovoltaic power generation is an excellent source of electrical power that results in much lower electricity bills, the power company will even refund you for the excess energy generated by your system if it is large enough. Building a grid tied solar power system is a relatively easy task. Given the large amount of government and electrical utility financial incentives that are available, it is a great time to join in the solar power revolution that is taking place in the world today.

- **Solar Photovoltaic Operation and Maintenance for Residential, Commercial, and Utility Systems:** This book details how to operate and maintain residential, commercial, and utility solar photovoltaic systems that are connected to the utility grid. By following the guidelines in this book you will be able to operate and maintain solar power systems that should give many years of reliable operation. Invaluable trouble shooting advice will aid in returning your system to full operation in the event of a problem.

- **Solar Photovoltaic DC Calculations for Residential, Commercial, and Utility Systems:** This book details how to run calculations for the DC circuit of solar photovoltaic systems. This would encompass residential, commercial, and utility systems that are connected to the utility grid. It covers the range of conditions that solar photovoltaic modules are exposed to throughout the year and shows how to incorporate these into an effective DC circuit that is well designed and reliable.

- **Solar Photovoltaic Resource for Residential, Commercial, and Utility Systems:** This book is a resource of information that is used in the solar photovoltaic field. This would encompass residential, commercial, and utility systems that are connected to the utility grid. It is a comprehensive collection of notes, diagrams, pictures and charts for a rapidly growing world of solar photovoltaic power generation technology. This book is illustrated in color.

Solar

- **Solar Irradiance and Insolation for Power Systems:** This book is a resource of information that is used in the solar power generation field. This would encompass residential, commercial, and utility systems that are connected to the utility grid. It is a comprehensive collection of notes, diagrams, pictures, and charts for a rapidly growing world of solar photovoltaic power generation technology. This book is illustrated in color.

- **Solar Site Selection for Power Systems:** This book is a comprehensive collection of images, diagrams, and notes that document the effects of light and heat in the solar power generation field. This would encompass residential, commercial, and utility systems that are connected to the utility grid. This is essential information for a rapidly growing world of solar power generation technology. This book is illustrated in color.

Architecture

- **Solar Reflections for Architects, Engineers, and Human Health:** This book is a comprehensive collection of images, diagrams, and notes that document the effects of sunlight in architecture. This is essential information for architects, engineers, and the medical profession. The discovery of the "Multiple-Sun" effect in architecture is detailed and this book is illustrated in color.

Human Health

- **Solar Radiation – A Cause of Illness and Cancer?** Illness and cancers have become part of our modern culture. It has been discovered that extremely high levels of man-made solar radiation exist in modern society. Could this be the one of the causes of illness and cancers? This book examines the increase in solar radiation and applies it to human health.
- **Solar Radiation, Global Warming, and Human Disease:** This book examines the modern development of the Earth and the potential impacts on global warming

and human disease. The destruction of the forests for modern agricultural use appears to have effects that are not fully understood and these are explored. Radiation deficiency and radiation overloading are investigated to see if they are factors in many illnesses and diseases.

- **Toxic Light:** Toxic Light takes a look at the light pollution that may be in your local environment and relates it to the health problems that it may cause. Light in the human environment is only just starting to be understood and something as innocent as your sunglasses may be able to make you ill! There are many examples of commonplace items in your environment that may have the ability to affect your health. Get ready for enlightenment about the most important human nutrient of light!

- **Toxic Health:** Toxic Health takes a look at the pollution that may be in your local environment and relates it to the health problems that it can cause. Pollution in the human environment is only just starting to be understood and something as innocent as light may be able to make you really ill! There are many examples of commonplace items in your environment that may have the ability to affect your health. In particular, we will investigate if modern city life is the most toxic thing of all to the modern human!

- **Toxic Electricity:** Random aches and pains? Fatigue? Insomnia? Facial pains? Irregular heartbeats? Sick kids? Relationship problems? Blotchy skin? Anxiety? Toxic electricity takes a look at the electrical system and asks the question: Is this one of the most toxic endeavors that humanity has ever engaged in?

Light Forensics © Steven Magee

Forensics

- **Electrical Forensics:** Electrical Forensics examines the many aspects of electricity, electronics and wireless communications that may lead to unusual behaviors to occur in humans. Electromagnetic interference is well known for its ability to affect mental functioning and human health. Electrical Forensics demonstrates how to identify toxic electromagnetic environments that may be the root cause of accidents and crimes.

- **Health Forensics:** Health Forensics examines the many aspects of modern society that may lead to unusual behaviors to occur in humans. Modern society has adopted habits that are well known for their ability to affect mental functioning and human health. Health Forensics demonstrates how to identify toxic human environments that may be the root cause of accidents and crimes.

- **Light Forensics:** Light Forensics examines the many aspects of modern lighting that may lead to unusual behaviors to occur in humans. Modern society has adopted optical products that are well known for their ability to affect mental functioning and human health. Light Forensics demonstrates how to identify toxic light that may be the root cause of accidents and crimes.

Religion

- **Solar Radiation, the Book of Revelations, and the Era of Light – Part 1:** Welcome to the Era of Light! Light has long been known to be essential nourishment for the human body. We will explore the different types of light that are present on Earth and relate it to human health and nature. Light is discussed extensively in the Bible and we will see if we can associate our findings to it.

Finally, we will investigate if the Industrial Revolution has created the ultimate toxin of poisonous sunlight!

Professional

- **Engineering Science and Education Journal Volume: 11, Issue: 4, Active Control Systems for Large Segmented Optical Mirrors:** A new generation of optical telescopes is on the drawing board. These will be true giants with primary mirrors having a diameter of up to 100 meters. The technology that will enable this revolution to take place was developed at the W. M. Keck Observatory in Hawaii, where the world's largest segmented mirrors are in daily use. This article looks at how the W. M. Keck Observatory proved the mirror technology that will be behind this new generation of telescopes.

You can search "Steven Magee Books" for the very latest publications.

www.youtube.com videos supporting the ideas in the books can be found by searching: StevenMageeBooks

"Life-transforming ideas have always come to me through books."
Bell Hooks

Light Forensics © Steven Magee

Book Reviews

Review by Lloyd Burrell on January 11, 2014 titled "Electrical Forensics – The Link Between EMF Exposures And Unusual Behaviors"

It's a fascinating and enlightening read. This book is information dense and there's plenty of pictures and diagrams to bring clarity. If you're interested in learning more about the health effects of EMFs with practical tips on mitigation I recommend reading Electrical Forensics.

Electrical Forensics rated 5 out of 5 stars.

Review by John Puccetti on October 27, 2013 titled "Dangers of electricity"

Steven has made many of the health problems of our century known in his book. But what will we do is this information? We live in a corporate dictatorship that masquerades as democracy.

Toxic Electricity rated 5 out of 5 stars.

Review by Sam Wieder on December 13, 2013 titled "A Most Illuminating, Educational, and Helpful Book"

Toxic Electricity provides a clear and comprehensive description of the many ways in which electrical fields impact human health and offers simple steps that anyone can take to live a more vibrant life in our electrically toxic world. The author does a masterful job of presenting some fairly complex concepts in a way that is easily understandable. Reading this book will give you a deeper understanding of how unseen radiation in your living and working environment may be impacting you. If you've been battling different health challenges or are chronically tired for no apparent reason, this book may very well open your eyes to some answers that will help you regain your health and your life.

Peter Sullivan @petermsullivan9 twittered on 10th December 2013:

@EnvironmentEMR Thanks for writing about the #autism / #EMF theory in you book Toxic Electricity. Also love the use of plants as "canaries".

Toxic Electricity: Eric Van rated it 5 out of 5 stars on Dec 23, 2012

If you think that you're home or work environment is safe and sound think again. If you are fatigued or have strange ailments currently or are concerned about cancer in the future then I recommend reading this book and getting an education into how you can avoid the toxins you receive from electricity.

Toxic Light rated 4 out of 5 Stars.

Review by John Puccetti on January 2, 2014 titled "Very technical".

I recommend you read "Tesla a man out of time" before you read this book. It is hard to grasp how much is wrong with radio frequencies and the electric grid and smart meters unless you really do some research first. But it is a wake up call to us all. Well worth reading.

"A good, sympathetic review is always a wonderful surprise."
Joyce Carol Oates

www.ingramcontent.com/pod-product-compliance
Lightning Source LLC
Chambersburg PA
CBHW051636170526
45167CB00001B/219